PRAYERS THAT AVAIL MUCH®

VOLUME 3

James 5:16

by
Germaine Copeland

And this is the confidence that we have in him, that, if we ask any thing according to his will, he heareth us: and if we know that he hear us, whatsoever we ask, we know that we have the petitions that we desired of him.

1 John 5:14,15

Harrison House
Tulsa, Oklahoma

Prayers That Avail Much®, *Volume 3*—
ISBN 1-57794-284-1
(Formerly ISBN 0-89274-939-3)
Copyright © 1996, 1997 by Word Ministries, Inc.

Germaine Copeland, President, Word Ministries, Inc.
38 Sloan Street
Roswell, Georgia 30075

Published by Harrison House, Inc.
P.O. Box 35035
Tulsa, Oklahoma 74153

Dedication

*T*his book is dedicated to the memory of my mother, Donnis Brock Griffin, the one who taught me the value of prayer. Her love for God and His people—her ministry and testimony—will abide forever.

Donnis Brock Griffin,
an intercessor
who worshiped her heavenly Father
in spirit and in truth.
May 2, 1915 - May 15, 1996

Contents

Part II: Group Prayers

Preface

*M*any of the prayers in this volume were written during the years just after I had served as pastor of Word of Life in Smyrna, Georgia. Originally, the church elected me to serve as its interim pastor. The faithfulness of God enabled me to remain steadfast in ministering to His people during my four-year tenure.

Having grown up in a pastor's home, I was familiar with church families and the challenges involved in pastoral ministry. The opportunities to increase in understanding and wisdom, to develop in the love of God and to grow in grace far exceeded my experiences as a minister's daughter.

After these years of taking on the cares of the church, I realized that I needed a time of refreshing and recreation. I had forgotten that I too needed ministry and had neglected my personal well-being. I began to understand how God truly watches over His Word to perform it in our lives (Jer. 1:12 AMP), as He began to introduce me to the breadth, length, depth and height of the love of the indwelling Christ. (Eph. 3:17-19.)

My life had been so controlled by the demands of a church that suddenly I found myself not knowing what to do next. It was time to regroup, and I didn't know where to begin. I felt drained of the life of God that had sustained me for the past twenty years of my life.

One day while I was seeking God for answers, the voice of the Father spoke to me: "Germaine, there isn't anything wrong with you spiritually; you need emotional healing." This was revelation to me, and I began to follow His leading on a new journey.

The engrafted Word brings about emotional healing—the salvation of the soul. (James 1:21.) It is my prayer that **...Christ through your faith [actually] dwell (settle down, abide, make His permanent home) in your hearts! May you be rooted deep in love and founded securely on love** (Eph. 3:17 AMP).

The freshness reflected in these special prayers has come about through spiritual renewal and emotional healing in my own life. It is my desire that you come before the Father as a little child, ever learning, growing and achieving. May you be blessed and encouraged as you read the prayers until they become your own—a reality in your life.

Germaine Copeland
President and Founder
Word Ministries, Inc.

Acknowledgments

*T*his book would not have been written without the prayers, encouragement and support of many people.

Once again, I express my appreciation to the editorial and author relations staff at Harrison House for their hard work, time and understanding.

My heartfelt appreciation and prayers go to the singles' group at Christian Growth Center in Christiansburg, Virginia, who submitted a list of prayer needs. They have been faithfully praying for the writing of the prayers for the singles' section of this work. In return, it is my prayer that every person will recognize his or her completeness and wholeness in Christ Jesus our Lord.

Many thanks to Pastors Rob and Tricia Sowell for their support and confidence in God's anointing that abides within me to write prayers that avail much.

A big thank-you to my friends, Mr. and Mrs. Joseph "Jodey" Turley of Blacksburg, Virginia, for furnishing me with the serenity of their lakeside condominium in the mountains of western Virginia. It was there that I experienced the solitude necessary to hear from God as I prayed, read, researched and wrote prayers for this book. I pray that the Lord will bless them abundantly for this kindness, according to His promise in Matthew 10:41 AMP: **He who receives and welcomes and accepts a prophet because he is a prophet shall receive a prophet's reward, and he who receives and welcomes and accepts a righteous man because he is a righteous man shall receive a righteous man's reward.**

I offer my gratitude and speak blessings to a special person, Mrs. Janice Miller of Kennesaw, Georgia, who has faithfully researched the Scriptures for God's answers to the special needs of so many people: Janice, **...God is not unrighteous to forget or overlook your labor and the love which you have shown for His name's sake in ministering to the needs of the saints (His own consecrated people), as you still do** (Heb. 6:10 AMP). **Now** [I commit you] **to Him Who, by (in consequence of) the [action of His] power that is at work within** [you], **is able to [carry out His purpose and] do superabundantly, far over and above all that** [you] **[dare] ask or think [infinitely beyond** [your] **highest prayers, desires, thoughts, hopes, or dreams]**—(Eph. 3:20 AMP).

My heart overflows with thanksgiving for those who have committed to pray for me. To my personal prayer partners: **Beloved, I pray that you may prosper in every way and [that your body] may keep well, even as [I know] your soul keeps well and prospers** (3 John 2 AMP). You have faithfully prayed for me, the Word Ministries staff and the development of this work—for continued traveling mercies and ministry to others, for my family and personal concerns. You too will be richly rewarded, in accordance with the promise of God: **The Lord gives the word [of power]; the women who bear and publish [the news] are a great host. The kings of the enemies' armies, they flee, they flee! She who tarries at home divides the spoil [left behind]** (Ps. 68:11,12 AMP).

Last, but not least, a big thank-you to my staff who have gone beyond the call of duty. They have worked extra hours to assist me in completing this volume. Jan Duncan, business administrator and director of Prayers That Avail Much International; Pat Horton, prayer coordinator and contributing writer for "The Good News Report"; Linda Lakomiak, circulation; and Donna Walker, editor and prayer request correspondent—each has written material for these prayers. God has blessed me with the right people with the right skills! To Him be the glory!

Introduction

*P*rayer is one of the most vital tools for success in every area of life.

In Matthew 6:6 AMP Jesus said, **But when you pray, go into your [most] private room, and, closing the door, pray to your Father, Who is in secret; and your Father, Who sees in secret, will reward you in the open.**

Even though much of our praying is intercessory prayer—praying for others—we receive personal rewards, such as building ourselves up on our most holy faith, praying in the Holy Ghost. (Jude 20.) These rewards include the constant ministry of transformation by the Holy Spirit—creating changes in us, bringing us into the reality of completeness in Christ Jesus and influencing others for good.

Prayer is relationship, and in this relationship the Christian finds himself involved in a process known as renewing the mind (Rom. 12:2)—putting off and discarding old thought patterns that hold him in bondage. *The Amplified Bible* tells us to **...[put off and discard [our] old unrenewed self]....** This is a process which requires that we **...be constantly renewed in the spirit of** [our] **mind [having a fresh mental and spiritual attitude],** and that we **...put on the new nature (the regenerate self) created** in God's image, [Godlike] in true righteousness and holiness (Eph. 4:22-24 AMP).

Praying scriptural prayers can drive out fear, worry, fretfulness, anxiety, unforgiveness, resentment and feelings of insecurity—by casting down every thought that would exalt itself against the knowledge of God. (2 Cor. 10:5.)

When you pray scriptural prayers, you pray with confidence, knowing that you are asking according to God's will, in agreement with His own plan. (1 John 5:14,15 AMP.)

When you pray in accordance with God's Word, your tongue becomes **...like the pen of a ready writer** (Ps. 45:1 AMP)—writing on the tablet of your heart.

What are you praying? Are you praying your will or God's will? Are you seeking **...(aim**[ing] **at and striv**[ing] **after) first of all His kingdom and His righteousness (His way of doing and being right)...?** If so, Jesus has promised, **...then all these things taken together will be given you besides** (Matt. 6:33 AMP).

Out of the abundance of the heart the mouth speaks. (Luke 6:45.) Your words outside the prayer closet must line up with the words you pray in secret. The prayer of faith changes things (James 5:16), and your faith must be accompanied by corresponding action, or behavior. (James 2:17 AMP.)

Praying scriptural prayers requires that we seek, explore, search, pursue and try to find God's answers for everyday situations. We begin by asking for godly wisdom—comprehensive insight into the ways and purposes of God. (Prov. 4:11 AMP.)

It is my prayer that

...you may be filled with the full (deep and clear) knowledge of His will in all spiritual wisdom [in comprehensive insight into the ways and purposes of God] and in understanding and discernment of spiritual things—that you may walk (live and conduct your[self]) in a manner worthy of the Lord, fully pleasing to Him and desiring to please Him in all things, bearing fruit in every good work and steadily growing and increasing in and by the knowledge of God [with fuller, deeper, and clearer insight, acquaintance, and recognition].

...that you may be invigorated and strengthened with all power according to the might of His glory, [to exercise] every kind of endurance and patience (perseverance and forbearance) with joy.

Colossians 1:9-11 AMP

As you prayerfully pursue the Lord, you will witness powerful answers to your prayers. Your prayer life will become fruitful and bring glory to your heavenly Father. He hears and answers prayers that are prayed according to His will and purpose and plan. (1 John 5:14,15.) His ears are open to the prayers of the righteous. (1 Pet. 3:12.)

Do not resist change. God is at work. Purpose that you will not **...let the world around you squeeze you into its own mould, but let God re-make you so that your whole attitude of mind is changed. Thus you will prove in practice that the will of God's good, acceptable to him and perfect** (Rom. 12:2 PHILLIPS). Prayer will no longer be a drudgery but a privilege as you become more and more intimately acquainted with the One Who loves you and gave Himself for you. (Gal. 2:20.)

PART I

Personal Prayers

Needs and Concerns
of the Individual

1

Submitting All to God

*F*ather, You are the Supreme Authority—a God of order. You have instituted other authority structures that will support healthy relationships and maintain harmony. It is my decision to surrender my will to You, that I might find protection and dwell in the secret place of the Most High.

Father, thank You for pastors and leaders of the church—those who are submitted to You and are examples to the congregation. I submit to the church elders (the ministers and spiritual guides of the church)—[giving them due respect and yielding to their counsel].

Lord, You know just how rebellious I have been. I ask Your forgiveness for manipulating circumstances and people—for trying to manipulate You to get my own way. May Your will be done in my life, even as it is in heaven.

Father, my life is out of control, and I submit myself to You. I resist the devil, and he will flee from me.

Obedience is far better than sacrifice. Father, You are much more interested in my listening to You than in my offerings of material things to You. Rebellion is as bad as the sin of witchcraft, and stubbornness is as bad as worshiping idols. Forgive me for practicing witchcraft and worshiping idols.

Father, You deserve honesty from the heart; yes, utter sincerity and truthfulness. Oh, give me this wisdom. Sprinkle me with the cleansing blood, and I shall be clean again. Wash me, and I shall be whiter than snow. You have rescued me from the dominion of darkness and brought me into the Kingdom of the Son You love, in Whom I have redemption, the forgiveness of sins.

Lord, I want to follow You. I am putting aside my own desires and conveniences. I yield my desires that are not in Your plan for me. Even in the midst of my fear I surrender and entrust my future to You. I choose to take up my cross and follow You [cleave steadfastly to You, conforming wholly to Your example in living and, if need be, in dying also]. I desire to lose my [lower life] on Your account that I might find it [the higher life].

Father, You gave Jesus to be my Example. He has returned to You, Father, and has sent the Holy Spirit to be my Helper and Guide. In this world there are temptations, trials and tribulations; but Jesus has overcome the world, and I am of good cheer.

Jesus is my Lord. I choose to become His servant. He calls me His friend.

Lord, help me to walk through the process of surrendering my all to You. I exchange rebellion and stubbornness for a willing and obedient heart. When I refuse to listen, anoint my ears to hear; when I am blinded by my own desires, open my eyes to see.

I belong to Jesus Christ, the Anointed One Who breaks down and destroys every yoke of bondage. In His name and in obedience to Your will, Father, I submit to the control and direction of the Holy Spirit Whom You have sent to live in me. I am Your child. All to You I surrender. I am an overcomer by the blood of the Lamb and by the word of my testimony!

In Jesus' name I pray, amen.

Scripture References

1 Corinthians 14:33	Psalm 51:6,7 TLB
1 Timothy 2:2	Colossians 1:13,14 NIV
Psalm 91:1	Matthew 10:38,39 AMP
1 Peter 5:5 AMP	John 16:33
Matthew 6:10	John 15:15
James 4:7	Revelation 12:11
1 Samuel 15:22,23 TLB	

2

Receiving Forgiveness

*F*ather, Your Word declares that if I ask for forgiveness, You will forgive me and cleanse me from all unrighteousness. Help me to believe; help me to receive my forgiveness for past and present sins. Help me to forgive myself. I confess Jesus as my Lord and believe in my heart that You raised Him from the dead, and I am saved.

Father, Your Son, Jesus, said that whatever I ask for in prayer, having faith and really believing, I will receive. Lord, I believe; help my unbelief.

Father, I count myself blessed, how happy I am—I get a fresh start, my slate's wiped clean. I count myself blessed (happy, fortunate, to be envied)—You, Father, are holding nothing against me and You're not holding anything back from me.

When I keep it all inside, my bones turn to powder, my words become daylong groans. The pressure never lets up; all the juices of my life dry up. I am letting it all out; I am saying once and for all that I am making a clean breast of my failures to You, Lord.

In the face of this feeling of guilt and unworthiness, I receive my forgiveness, and the pressure is gone—my guilt dissolved, my sin disappeared. I am blessed, for You have forgiven my transgressions—You have covered my sins. I am blessed, for You will never count my sins against me.

Father, You chose me [actually picked me out for Yourself as Your very own] in Christ before the foundation of the world, that I should be holy (consecrated and set apart for You), blameless in Your sight, even above reproach, before You in love. In Jesus I have redemption (deliverance and salvation) through His blood, the remission (forgiveness) of my offenses (shortcomings and trespasses), in accordance with the riches and the generosity of Your gracious favor.

Lord, I have received Your Son, Jesus. I believe in His name, and He has given me the right to become Your child. I acknowledge You, Lord, as my Father. Thank You for forgiving me and absolving me of all guilt. I am an overcomer by the blood of the Lamb and by the word of my testimony.

In the name of Jesus, amen.

Scripture References

1 John 1:9	*Psalm 32:1-6 MESSAGE*
Romans 10:9,10	*Romans 4:7,8 NIV*
Mark 11:23	*Ephesians 1:4,7 AMP*
Matthew 21:22 AMP	*John 1:12 NIV*
Mark 9:24	*Revelation 12:11*
Psalm 32:1 AMP	

3

Walking in Humility

*F*ather, I clothe myself with humility [as the garb of a servant, so that its covering cannot possibly be stripped from me]. I renounce pride and arrogance. Father, You give grace to the humble. Therefore I humble myself under Your mighty hand, that in due time You may exalt me.

In the name of Jesus, I cast the whole of my care [all my anxieties, all my worries, all my concerns for my future, once and for all] on You, for You care for me affectionately and care about me watchfully. I expect a life of victory and awesome deeds because my actions are done on behalf of a spirit humbly submitted to Your truth and righteousness.

Father, in the name of Jesus, I refuse to be wise in my own eyes; but I choose to fear You and shun evil. This will bring health to my body and nourishment to my bones.

Father, I humble myself and submit to Your Word that speaks—exposes, sifts, analyzes and judges the very thoughts and purposes of my heart. I test my own actions, so that I might have appropriate self-esteem, without comparing myself to anyone else. The security of Your guidance will allow me to carry my own load with energy and confidence.

I listen carefully and hear what is being said to me. I incline my ear to wisdom and apply my heart to understanding and insight. Humility and fear of You bring wealth and honor and life.

Father, I hide Your Word in my heart, that I might not sin against You. As one of Your chosen people, holy and dearly loved, I clothe myself with compassion, kindness, humility, gentleness and patience. I bear with others and forgive whatever grievances I may have against anyone. I forgive as You forgave me. And over all these virtues I put on love, which binds them all together in perfect unity. I let the peace of Christ rule in my heart, and I am thankful for Your grace and the power of the Holy Spirit.

Father, may Your will be done on earth in my life as it is in heaven.

In Jesus' name, amen.

Scripture References

1 Peter 5:5-7 AMP	*Proverbs 22:4* NIV
Proverbs 3:7,8 NIV	*Psalm 119:11*
Hebrews 4:12 AMP	*Colossians 3:12-15* NIV
Galatians 6:4,5 NIV	*Matthew 6:10* NIV
Proverbs 2:2 NIV	

4

Giving Thanks to God

Introduction

*G*od saw you when you were in your mother's womb. (Ps. 139:13-16.) He knew your mother and father and the circumstances of the home where you were to grow up. He knew the schools you would attend and the neighborhood in which you would live.

God gave you the ability to survive and walked with you through good times and bad. He gave you survival techniques and guardian angels to keep and protect you. (Ps. 91:11.) He chose you before the foundation of the world to be holy and without blame before Him in love. (Eph. 1:4.)

He cried with you when you cried. He laughed with you when you laughed. He was grieved when you were misunderstood and treated unfairly. He watched and waited, looking forward to the day when You would receive Jesus as Your Savior. To as many as received Him gave He the power, the right and the authority to become the sons of God. (John 1:12 AMP.) He longs for your fellowship, desiring for you to know Him more and more intimately.

Your survival techniques were probably different than mine. Whatever they were, and whatever your life may have been like up to this point, the peace of God can change the regrets and the wounds of the past into thanksgiving and praise. You can experience wholeness by earnestly and sincerely praying this prayer.

I.

Daily Prayer of Thanksgiving

Father, I come to You in the name of Jesus. With the help of the Holy Spirit and by Your grace, I join with the heavenly host, making a joyful noise to You and serving You with gladness! I come before Your presence with singing!

Lord, I know (perceive, recognize and understand with approval) that You are God! It is You Who made us, not we ourselves [and we are Yours]! We are Your people and the sheep of Your pasture.

Father, I enter into Your gates with thanksgiving and present an offering of thanks. I enter into Your courts with praise! I am thankful and delight to say so. I bless and affectionately praise Your name! For You are good and Your mercy and loving-kindness are everlasting. Your faithfulness and truth endure to all generations. It is a good and delightful thing to give thanks to You, O Most High.

Lord, by Your Holy Spirit perfect the fruit of my lips. Help me draw thanksgiving forth from my innermost resources; reach down into the most secret places of my heart, that I may offer significant thanksgiving to You, Father.

Thank You for my parents, who gave me life. I am grateful for the victories and achievements I have experienced in spite of my hurts—the bruises and the abuses that boxed me in when I was a small child. You used them for good even though Satan intended them for my destruction.

You prepared me to listen to the inner voice—the voice of Your Holy Spirit.

Thank You for Your grace, which is teaching me to trust myself and others. Thank You for life—life in all its abundance.

It was You Who gave me a desire to pray, and I am grateful for the prayer closet where we meet, and I thank You for Your Word. Life is exciting, and I am grateful that I am alive for such a time as this.

Thank You for past and present relationships. I learn from those who oppose me and from those who are for me. You taught me to recognize and understand my strengths and weaknesses. You gave me discernment and spiritual understanding. I enter Your gates with thanksgiving in my heart.

You are my Father. I am your child, loved by You unconditionally. I rejoice in You, Lord, and give thanks at the remembrance of Your holiness.

I am an overcomer by the blood of the Lamb and by the word of my testimony.

In the name of Jesus, amen.

Scripture References

Psalm 100:1-5 AMP	Philippians 2:13
Psalm 92:1 AMP	Esther 4:14
Psalm 138:8	Psalm 100:4
Hebrews 13:15	Philippians 3:1
Genesis 50:20 NIV	Psalm 30:4
John 10:10	Revelation 12:11

II.

Prayer of Thanksgiving for Food Eaten While Traveling

Father, I ask for the wisdom to order that which is healthy and nourishing to my body.

In the name of Jesus, I resist the lust of the flesh and the lust of the eye as I scan the menu. When I am in doubt about what I am to order, I will pause and ask for wisdom, which You will give generously without finding fault with me.

Should I unknowingly eat or drink any deadly thing, it will not harm me, for the Spirit of life makes me free from the law of sin and death.

Everything You have created, Father, is good, and nothing is to be thrown away or refused if it is received with thanksgiving. It is hallowed and consecrated by Your Word and by prayer.

I receive this food with thanksgiving and will eat the amount that is sufficient for me.

In the name of Jesus, amen.

Scripture References

James 1:5	Romans 8:2
1 John 2:16	1 Timothy 4:4,5 AMP
Mark 16:18	Psalm 136:1,25

5

Committing to a Fast

I.

Beginning a Fast

Introduction

*T*here are different kinds of fasts: a total fast from foods and liquids for a short interval of time; a liquid fast, in which only water may be drunk; a juice fast, which involves drinking water and a given amount of juices at normal meal times; a fast from meats, in which only fruits and vegetables may be eaten.

It is important to understand the effects of fasting on the spirit, soul and body. Before committing to a fast, I encourage you to study the Word of God and to read books that provide important nutritional and other health information. Understanding will help to avoid harm and injury— both physically and spiritually.

Do not flaunt your fast, but do talk with your family and close associates if necessary to let them know what you are doing.

(Personal note: During times of fasting I continue to prepare meals at home for my family.)

Prayer

Father, I consecrate this fast to You and set my mind to gain understanding in these matters for which I am concerned. *(Write your concerns out and keep them before your eyes. Do not lose sight of the reason for your fast.)*

I humble myself before You, Most High God. In accordance with Daniel 10:1-3, I will eat no _____ for the period of _____.

I obey the words of Jesus by putting on festive clothing, so that no one will suspect that I am fasting.

Father, You know every secret, and I look to You for my reward. I am assured that You hear me when I pray according to Your will, and I know that I shall have the petitions that I desire of You.

Father, I delight myself in You, and You cause my desires to be agreeable with Your will.

I choose the fast You have chosen: to loose the chains of injustice and untie the cords of the yoke, to set the oppressed free and to break every yoke. I share my food with the hungry and provide the poor wanderer with shelter. When I see the naked, I will clothe him; and I will not turn away from my own flesh and blood. Then my light will break forth like the dawn, and my healing will quickly appear; then my righteousness will go before me, and Your glory, Lord, will be my rear guard.

Father, thank You for cleansing me—spirit, soul and body. All my ways seem innocent to me, but my motives are weighed by You, my Lord and my Master. I commit this fast to You, and my plans will succeed. I thank You that it is You Who give the wise answer of the tongue.

Forever, O Lord, Your Word stands firm in heaven. Your faithfulness extends to every generation, like the earth You created; it endures by Your decree, for everything serves Your plans.

In Jesus' name, amen.

Scripture References

Matthew 6:17,18 TLB	1 Thessalonians 5:23
1 John 5:14,15	Proverbs 16:2,3 NIV
Psalm 37:4	Proverbs 16:1

Proverbs 16:3 AMP   *Psalm 119:89-91* TLB

Isaiah 58:6-8 TLB

II.

Ending a Fast

Introduction

It is best to break a fast by eating fruit, broth or a light salad, gradually adding other foods day by day depending upon the length of the fast.

Prayer

Father, in the name of Jesus, You are my Light and my Salvation; whom shall I fear? You are the Strength of my life; of whom shall I be afraid?

Father, You have given me the desires of my heart. You have heard and answered my prayer. To You be the glory! Great things You have done!

I rest in You, awaiting the manifestation of all that I required and inquired of You.

I thank You for giving me Your strength to face each day full of sap [of spiritual vitality]. Today, I break this fast as You have directed. I thank You for this food because it is consecrated by Your Word and prayer.

In Jesus' name, amen.

Scripture References

Psalm 27:1   Psalm 92:14 AMP

Psalm 37:4   1 Timothy 4:4,5 AMP

Psalm 34:4 AMP

6

Pleading the Blood of Jesus

I.

Morning Prayer [1]

*F*ather, I come in the name of Jesus to plead His blood on my life and on all that belongs to me and on all over which You have made me a steward.

I plead the blood of Jesus on the portals of my mind, my body (the temple of the Holy Spirit), my emotions and my will. I believe that I am protected by the blood of the Lamb that gives me access to the Holy of Holies.

I plead the blood on my children, my grandchildren and their children and on all those whom You have given me in this life.

---

[1] Based on a prayer written by Joyce Meyer in *The Word, the Name and the Blood* (Tulsa: Harrison House, 1995).

Lord, You have said that the life of the flesh is in the blood. Thank You for this blood that has cleansed me from sin and sealed the New Covenant, of which I am a partaker.

In Jesus' name, amen.

Scripture References

Exodus 12:7,13	Leviticus 17:11
1 Corinthians 6:19	1 John 1:7
Hebrews 9:6-14	Hebrews 13:20 AMP

II.

Evening Prayer[2]

Father, as I lie down to sleep, I plead the blood of Jesus upon my life—within me, around me and between me and all evil and the author of evil.

In Jesus' name, amen.

---

[2] Based on a prayer written by Mrs. C. Nuzum as recorded by Billye Brim in *The Blood and The Glory* (Tulsa: Harrison House, 1995).

7

Handling the Day of Trouble or Calamity

Introduction

During a time of trouble or calamity, it is sometimes difficult to remember the promises of God. The pressures of the moment may seem overwhelming. At such times, it is often helpful to read, meditate on and pray the entire chapter of Psalm 91.

It may be that during a stressful time you will find this entire prayer too long. If so, draw from the Scriptures included in the following prayer. You may find yourself praying one paragraph or reading it aloud to yourself or to your family and friends.

I also encourage you to meditate on this prayer during good times.

At all times, remember that faith comes by hearing, and hearing by the Word of God. (Rom. 10:17.)

Prayer

Father, I come to You in the name of Jesus, acknowledging You as my Refuge and High Tower. You are a refuge and a stronghold in these times of trouble (high cost, destitution and desperation).

In the day of trouble You will hide me in Your shelter; in the secret place of Your tent will You hide me; You will set me high upon a rock. And now shall my head be lifted up above my enemies round about me; in Your tent I will offer sacrifices and shouting of joy; I will sing, yes, I will sing praises to You, O Lord. Hear, O Lord, when I cry aloud; have mercy and be gracious to me and answer me!

On the authority of Your Word, I declare that I have been made the righteousness of God in Christ Jesus. When I cry for help, You, Lord, hear me and deliver me out of all my distress and troubles. You are close to me, for I am of a broken heart, and You save such as are crushed with sorrow for sin and are humbly and thoroughly penitent. Lord, many are the evils that confront me, but You deliver me out of them all.

Thank You for being merciful and gracious to me, O God, for my soul takes refuge and finds shelter and confidence in You; yes, in the shadow of Your wings I take refuge and am confident until calamities and destructive storms are passed. You perform on my behalf and reward me. You bring to pass Your purposes for me, and surely You complete them!

Father, You are my Refuge and Strength [mighty and impenetrable to temptation], a very present and well-proved help in trouble.

Lord, You have given and bequeathed to me Your peace. By Your grace I will not let my heart be troubled; neither will I let it be afraid. With the help of the Holy Spirit I will [stop allowing myself to be agitated and disturbed; and I refuse to permit myself to be fearful and intimidated and cowardly and unsettled].

By faith, I respond to these troubles and calamities: [I am full of joy now!] I exult and triumph in my troubles and rejoice in my sufferings, knowing that pressure and affliction and hardship produce patient and unswerving endurance. And endurance (fortitude) develops maturity of character (approved faith and tried integrity). And character [of this sort] produces [the habit of] joyful and confident hope of eternal salvation. Such hope never disappoints or deludes or shames me, for Your love has been poured out in my heart through the Holy Spirit, Who has been given to me.

In Jesus name, amen.

Scripture References

Psalm 9:9 AMP

Psalm 27:5-7 AMP

2 Corinthians 5:21

Psalm 34:17-20 AMP

Psalm 57:1,2 AMP

Psalm 46:1 AMP

John 14:27 AMP

Romans 5:3-5 AMP

8

Breaking the Curse of Abuse

Introduction

*C*hrist redeemed us from the curse of the law by becoming a curse for us, for it is written: "Cursed is everyone who is hung on a tree."

Galatians 3:13 NIV

On a Sunday morning after I had taught a lesson titled "Healing for the Emotionally Wounded," a young man wanted to speak with me. I listened intently as he told me that he had been in jail for physically abusing his family and was now on probation. His wife had filed for divorce, and he was living alone. It was not easy for him to confess his sin to me, and I was impressed by his humble attitude.

He said, "I am glad that this message is being given in the Church and the abused can receive ministry. Is there anywhere that the abuser can go to receive spiritual help?"

He shared with me that he was attending a support group for abusers. He desired to commit to a church where he could receive forgiveness and acceptance. He knew that any lasting change would have to be from the inside out by the Spirit. I prayed with him, but it would be three years before I could write a prayer for the abuser.

As I read, studied, and sought the Lord, I discovered that the abuser is usually a person who has been abused. Often, the problem is a generational curse that has been in the family of the abuser for as far back as anyone can remember. Many times the abuser declares that he will never treat his wife and children as he has been treated, but in spite of his resolve he finds himself reacting in the same violent manner.

The generational curse is reversed as the abuser is willing to allow God to remove the character flaws that have held him in bondage.

If you are an abuser, I encourage you to pray this prayer for yourself until it becomes a reality in your life. If you know someone who is an abuser, pray this as a prayer of intercession in the third person.

Prayer

I receive and confess that Jesus is my Lord, and I ask that Your will be done in my life.

Father, You have rescued me from the dominion of darkness and have brought me into the Kingdom of the Son of Your love. Once I was darkness, but now I am light in You; I walk as a child of light. The abuse is exposed and reproved by the light—it is made visible and clear; and where everything is visible and clear there is light.

Help me to grow in grace (undeserved favor, spiritual strength) and recognition and knowledge and understanding of my Lord and Savior, Jesus Christ, so that I may experience Your love and trust You to be a Father to me.

The history of my earthly family is filled with abusive behavior, much hatred, strife and rage. The painful memory of past abuse *(verbal, emotional, physical and/or sexual)* has caused me to be hostile and abusive to others.

I desire to be a doer of the Word and not a hearer only. No matter which way I turn, I can't make myself do right. I want to, but I can't. When I want to do good, I don't; and when I try not to do wrong, I do it anyway. It seems that sin still has me in its evil grasp. This pain has caused me to hurt myself and others. In my mind I want to be Your willing servant, but instead I find myself still enslaved to sin.

I confess my sin of abuse, resentment and hostility toward others, and I ask You to forgive me. You are faithful and just to forgive my sin and cleanse me from all unrighteousness. I am tired of reliving the past in my present life, perpetuating the generational curse of anger and abuse.

Jesus was made a curse for me; therefore, Lord, I put on Your whole armor, that I may be able to successfully stand against all the strategies and the tricks of the devil. I thank You that the evil power of abuse is broken, over-thrown and cast down. I submit myself to You and resist the devil. The need to hurt others no longer controls me or my family.

In Jesus' name, amen.

Scripture References

Romans 10:9

Romans 7:18-25 TLB

Matthew 6:10

1 John 1:9

Colossians 1:13 AMP

Galatians 3:13

Ephesians 5:8,13 AMP

Ephesians 6:11,12 TLB

2 Peter 3:18 AMP

2 Corinthians 10:5

James 1:22

James 4:7

9

Healing From Abuse

Introduction

*T*his prayer can be applied to any form of abuse—physical, mental, emotional or sexual. I wrote it after reading T. D. Jakes' book *Woman, Thou Art Loosed.*[1] By praying it, I personally have experienced victory and freedom—I am no longer a victim but an overcomer.

Prayer

Lord, You are my High Priest, and I ask You to loose me from this "infirmity." The abuse I suffered pronounced me guilty and condemned. I was bound—in an emotional prison—crippled and could in no wise lift up myself. You have called me to Yourself, and I have come.

The anointing that is upon You is present to bind up and heal the brokenness and emotional wounds of the past. You are the Truth that makes me free.

---

[1] (Shippensburg, PA: Treasure House, 1993).

Thank You, Lord, for guiding me through the steps to emotional wholeness. You have begun a good work in me, and You will perform it until the day of Christ Jesus.

Father, I desire to live according to the Spirit of life in Christ Jesus. This Spirit of life in Christ, like a strong wind, has magnificently cleared the air, freeing me from a fated lifetime of brutal tyranny at the hands of abuse.

Since I am now free, it is my desire to forget those things that lie behind and strain forward to what lies ahead. I press on toward the goal to win the [supreme and heavenly] prize to which You in Christ Jesus are calling me upward. The past will no longer control my thinking patterns or my behavior.

Praise be to You! I am a new creature in Christ Jesus. Old things have passed away; and, behold, all things have become new. I declare and decree that henceforth I will walk in newness of life.

Forgive me, Father, for self-hatred and self-condemnation. I am Your child. You sent Jesus that I might have life and have it more abundantly. Thank You for the blood of Jesus, which makes me whole.

It is my desire to throw all spoiled virtue and cancerous evil in the garbage. In simple humility, I let my Gardener, You Lord, landscape me with the Word, making a salvation-garden of my life.

Father, by Your grace, I forgive my abuser(s) and ask You to bring him/her/them to repentance.

In the name of Jesus I pray. Amen.

Scripture References

Luke 13:11,12	*Romans 6:4*
John 14:6	*1 John 3:1,2*
John 8:32	*John 10:10*
Philippians 1:6	*1 John 1:7*
Romans 8:2 MESSAGE	*James 1:21 MESSAGE*
Philippians 3:13,14 AMP	*Matthew 5:44*
2 Corinthians 5:17	*2 Peter 3:9*

10

Letting Go of the Past

*F*ather, I realize my helplessness in saving myself, and I glory in what Christ Jesus has done for me. I let go—put aside all past sources of my confidence—counting them worth less than nothing, in order that I may experience Christ and become one with Him.

Lord, I have received Your Son, and He has given me the authority (power, privilege and right) to become Your child.

I unfold my past and put into proper perspective those things that are behind. I have been crucified with Christ, and I no longer live, but Christ lives in me. The life I live in the body, I live by faith in the Son of God, Who loved me and gave Himself for me. I trust in You, Lord, with all my heart and lean not on my own understanding. In all my ways I acknowledge You, and You will make my paths straight.

I want to know Christ and the power of His resurrection and the fellowship of sharing in His sufferings, becoming like Him in His death, and so, somehow, to attain to the resurrection from the dead. So, whatever it takes, I will be one who lives in the fresh newness of life of those who are alive from the dead.

I don't mean to say that I am perfect. I haven't learned all I should, but I keep working toward that day when I will finally be all that Christ saved me for and wants me to be.

I am bringing all my energies to bear on this one thing: Regardless of my past I look forward to what lies ahead. I strain to reach the end of the race and receive the prize for which You are calling me up to heaven because of what Christ Jesus did for me.

In His name I pray, amen.

Scripture References

Philippians 3:7-9 TLB   Proverbs 3:5,6 NIV

John 1:12 AMP   Philippians 3:10,11 NIV

Psalm 32:5 AMP   Romans 6:4

Philippians 3:13   Philippians 3:12-14 TLB

Galatians 2:20 NIV

11

Casting Down Imaginations

*F*ather, though I live in the world, I do not wage war as the world does. The weapons I fight with are not the weapons of the world. On the contrary, they have divine power to demolish strongholds. I demolish arguments and every pretension that sets itself up against the knowledge of You, and I take captive every thought to make it obedient to Christ.

In the name of Jesus, I ask You, Father, to bless those who have despitefully used me. Whenever I feel afraid, I will trust in You. When I feel miserable, I will express thanksgiving; and when I feel that life is unfair, I will remember that You are more than enough.

When I feel ashamed, help me to remember that I no longer have to be afraid; I will not suffer shame. I am delivered from the fear of disgrace; I will not be humiliated. I relinquish the shame of my youth.

It is well with my soul, for You have redeemed me. You have called me by my name.

I am in Your will for my life at this time. I am being transformed through the renewing of my mind. I am able to test and approve [for myself] what Your will is—Your good and acceptable and perfect will.

You have good things reserved for my future. All my needs will be met according to Your riches in glory. I will replace worry for my family with asking You to protect and care for them.

You are love, and perfect love casts out fear.

In Jesus' name, amen.

Scripture References

2 Corinthians 10:3-5 NIV   Romans 12:2 AMP

Luke 6:28   Jeremiah 29:11 AMP

Isaiah 54:4 NIV   Philippians 4:19

Isaiah 43:1   1 Peter 5:7

Romans 12:2   1 John 4:8,18

12

Overcoming Fear

Introduction

"... *Y*ou **will know the truth, and the truth will set you free."**

John 8:32 NIV

This prayer was written by someone who faced her worst fears and overcame them through faith. She is an enforcer of the triumphant victory of Jesus in her speech and actions. It is He Who has spoiled principalities and powers, making a show of them openly. (Col. 2:15.)

The writer of this prayer was convinced that neither death nor life, neither angels nor demons, neither the present nor the future, nor any powers, neither height nor depth, nor anything else in all creation, would be able to separate her from the love of God that is in Christ Jesus our Lord. (Rom. 8:38,39 NIV.)

Make that truth the foundation of your faith as you pray the following prayer to overcome fear of any kind in your life.

Prayer

Father, Your Word is a lamp to my feet and a light to my path.

Lord, investigate my life; get all the facts firsthand. I'm an open book to You; even from a distance, You know what I'm thinking.

You know when I leave and when I get back; I'm never out of Your sight. You know everything I'm going to say before I start the first sentence. I look behind me and You're there, then up ahead and You're there, too—Your reassuring presence, coming and going. This is too much, too wonderful—I can't take it all in!

Is there any place I can go to avoid Your Spirit? to be out of Your sight? If I climb to the sky, You're there! If I go underground, You're there! If I flew on morning's wings to the far western horizon, You'd find me in a minute—You're already there waiting!

Then I said to myself, "Oh, He even sees me in the dark! At night I'm immersed in the light!" It's a fact: Darkness isn't dark to You; night and day, darkness and light—they're all the same to You.

Father, I will not be anxious about anything, but in every circumstance by prayer and petition with a thankful heart I will make my wishes known to You. I receive Your peace and allow Your peace, which passes all understanding, to rule over my heart and mind as I rest in You.

Empowered by the Holy Spirit, I am not moved or shaken; I do not fear bad news: my heart is steadfast trusting in You, Lord. You have established my heart, making it secure and steady. You are with me, and You strengthen me; I will not be afraid.

Father, You have not given me a spirit of fear, but of power, and of love, and of a sound mind. You are my Deliverer from all fear. I thank You that I am set free from the fear of rejection and ridicule. I am not intimidated by others, because You, Lord, are my Helper; I am not seized with alarm: [I will not fear or dread or be terrified]. What can man do to me?

In everything that I encounter in this life, I am an overcomer by the blood of the Lamb and by the word of my testimony.

In the name of Jesus, amen.

Scripture References

Psalm 119:105 *AMP*	Isaiah 41:10 *TLB*
Psalm 139:1-12 *MESSAGE*	2 Timothy 1:7
Philippians 4:6,7 *AMP*	Psalm 34:4
Psalm 112:6-8 *TLB, AMP*	Hebrews 13:6 *AMP*
Psalm 27:1	Revelation 12:11

13

Overcoming a Feeling of Abandonment

Introduction

When my father and my mother forsake me, then the Lord will take me up.

Psalm 27:10

This prayer was prompted by a letter I received from someone who is incarcerated. According to his letter, he grew up in a family of fighters and felt abandoned by his family and so-called friends. His pugnacious attitude controlled him, and eventually his aggressive temperament caused him to almost kill someone.

In prison he was ridiculed and harassed by inmates who encouraged him to fight. His wife divorced him, and again he was left alone. Thoughts that "no one likes me" continually tormented him, but he desired to know how to change his thinking.

A laborer of the harvest introduced him to Jesus and my book *Prayers That Avail Much, Volume 1.*[1] He still had trouble controlling his temper even with those who might have been his friends. His letter was filled with the pain of loneliness and abandonment. The following is a revised and expanded version of the original prayer I wrote encouraging him to pray for himself.

Prayer

Father, I have confessed Jesus as my Lord and believe in my heart that You raised Him from the dead. I ask for the power of the Holy Spirit to overcome the resentment I feel towards those who abused and abandoned me.

Now, I am Your child. When other people leave me and I feel unloved, I am thankful that You will never, ever leave me alone or reject me.

Jesus gave His life for me and called me His friend. He lives in my heart, and I am on my way to heaven. That is plenty to be thankful for. So when I am lonely or discouraged, I can think of things that are pure and holy and good, even when I am apart from everyone.

Heavenly Father, I ask You to strengthen me and help me while in the presence of the dangers surrounding

---

[1] Tulsa: Harrison House, 1989, 1997.

me. You have assigned angels who will accompany, defend and preserve me in all my ways [of obedience and service]. I am not alone. Your Word says that there is nothing that can separate me from the love of Christ—not pain nor stress nor persecution. I will come to the top of every circumstance or trial through Jesus' love.

You are concerned with the smallest detail that concerns me, and You are my Help. I ask You for friends who will admonish and encourage me. Teach me how to trust others and be a friend who sticks closer than a brother. Help me to walk in Your love and show myself friendly.

In Jesus' name, amen.

Scripture References

Romans 10:9,10 NIV   *Psalm 91:11 AMP*

Hebrews 13:5 NIV   *Romans 8:35,39*

John 15:13-15 NIV   *Psalm 138:8 AMP*

1 Thessalonians 5:18 TLB   *Psalm 46:1 MESSAGE*

Philippians 4:8 TLB   *Proverbs 18:24*

Isaiah 41:10 TLB

14

Overcoming Discouragement

Introduction

*M*oses returned to the Lord and said, "O Lord, why have you brought trouble upon this people? Is this why you sent me? Ever since I went to Pharaoh to speak in your name, he has brought trouble upon this people, and you have not rescued your people at all."

Exodus 5:22,23 NIV

Here in this passage, we find Moses discouraged, complaining to God.

It is important that we approach God with integrity in an attitude of humility. But because we fear making a negative confession, we sometimes cross the line of honesty into the line of denial and delusion. Let's be honest. God already knows what we are feeling. He can handle our anger, complaints and disappointments. He understands us. He is aware of our human frailties (Ps. 103:14) and can be touched with the feelings of our infirmities. (Heb. 4:15.)

Whether your "trouble" is a business failure, abandonment, depression, mental disorder, chemical imbalance, oppression, a marriage problem, a child who is in a strange land of drugs and alcohol, financial disaster or anything else, the following prayer is for you.

Sometimes when you are in the midst of discouragement it is difficult to remember that you have ever known any Scripture. I admonish you to read this prayer aloud until you recognize the reality of God's Word in your spirit, soul and body. Remember, God is watching over His Word to perform it. (Jer. 1:12 AMP.) He will perfect that which concerns you. (Ps. 138:8.)

Prayer

Lord, I do not understand why You have allowed this trouble to assail me. It was after I began to follow You in obedience that this trouble was manifested in my life. I have exhausted all my possibilities for changing my situation and circumstances and have found that I am powerless to change. I believe; help me overcome my unbelief. All things are not possible with man, but all things are possible with You. I humble myself before You, and You will lift me up.

I have a great High Priest Who has gone through the heavens: Jesus, Your Son. And I hold firmly to the faith I profess. My High Priest is able to sympathize with my weaknesses. He was tempted in every way, just as I am—yet was without sin. I approach Your throne of grace with confidence, so that I may receive mercy and find grace to help me in my time of need.

In the face of discouragement, disappointment and anger, I choose to believe that Your word to Moses is Your word to me. You are mighty to deliver. Because of Your mighty hand, You will drive out the forces that have set themselves up against me. You are the Lord, Yahweh, the Promise-Keeper, the Almighty One. You appeared to Abraham, to Isaac and to Jacob and established Your covenant with them.

Father, I believe that You have heard my groaning, my cries. I will live to see Your promises of deliverance fulfilled in my life. You have not forgotten one word of Your promise; You are a Covenant-Keeper.

It is You Who will bring me out from under the yoke of bondage and free me from being a slave to _____. You have redeemed me with an outstretched arm and with mighty acts of judgment. You have taken me as Your own, and You are my God. You are a Father to me. You have delivered me from the past that has held me in bondage and translated me into the Kingdom of love, peace, joy and righteousness. I will no longer settle for the pain of the past. Where sin abounds, grace does much more abound.

Father, what You have promised, I will go and possess, in the name of Jesus. I am willing to take the chance, to take the risk, to get back into the good fight of faith. It is with patient endurance and steady and active persistence that I run the race, the appointed course that is set before me. I rebuke the spirit of fear, for I am established in righteousness. Oppression and destruction shall not come near me. Behold, they may gather together and stir up strife, but it is not from You, Father. Whoever stirs up strife against me shall fall and surrender to me. I am more than a conqueror through Him Who loves me.

In His name I pray, amen.

Scripture References

*(This prayer is based on Exodus 5:22-6:11
and includes other verses where applicable.)*

Mark 9:24 NIV	Deuteronomy 26:8
Luke 18:27	Colossians 1:13
1 Peter 5:6 NIV	Romans 5:20
Hebrews 4:14-16 NIV	1 Timothy 6:12
Exodus 6:3,4 AMP	Hebrews 12:1 AMP
Genesis 49:22-26 AMP	Isaiah 54:14-16
1 Kings 8:56	Romans 8:37

15

Overcoming a Sense of Hopelessness

*F*ather, as Your child I boldly come before Your throne of grace, that I may receive mercy and find grace to help in this time of need.

Father, I know that Your ears are open to my prayers. I ask that You listen to my prayer, O God, and hide not Yourself from my supplication! I ask that You attend to me and answer me, for I am restless and distraught in my complaint and must moan. Fear and trembling have come upon me; horror and fright have overwhelmed me.

Oh, that I had wings like a dove! I would fly away and be at rest. Yes, I would wander far away; I would lodge in the wilderness. I would hasten to escape and to find a shelter from the stormy wind and tempest.

I am calling upon You, my God, to rescue me. You redeem my life in peace from the battle of hopelessness that is against me. I cast my burden on You, Lord, [releasing the weight of it], and You sustain me; You will never allow the [consistently] righteous to be moved (made to slip, fall or fail).

Hopelessness lies in wait for me, to swallow me up or trample me all day long. What time I am afraid, I will have confidence in and put my trust and reliance in You. By [Your help], God, I will praise Your Word; on You I lean, rely and confidently put my trust; I will not fear.

You know my every sleepless night. Each tear and heartache is answered with Your promise. I am thanking You with all my heart. You pulled me from the brink of death, my feet from the cliff-edge of doom. Now, I stroll at leisure with You in the sunlit fields of life.

[What, what would have become of me], Lord, had I not believed that I would see Your goodness in the land of the living! I wait and hope for and expect You; I am brave and of good courage, and I let my heart be stout and enduring. Yes, I wait for and hope for and expect You.

Father, I give You all my worries and cares, for You are always thinking about me and watching everything that concerns me. I am well balanced and careful—vigilant, watching out for attacks from Satan, my great enemy. By Your grace I am standing firm, trusting You, and I remember that other Christians all around the world are going through these sufferings too. You, God, are full of kindness through Christ and will give me Your eternal glory.

In the name of Jesus I am an overcomer by the blood of the Lamb and by the word of my testimony. Amen.

Scripture References

Hebrews 4:16

Psalm 55:1 MESSAGE

Psalm 55:1,2 AMP

Psalm 55:5-8 AMP

Psalm 55:16,18,22 AMP

Psalm 56:2-4 AMP

Psalm 56:5,8 MESSAGE

Psalm 56:13 MESSAGE

Psalm 27:13,14 AMP

1 Peter 5:7-9 AMP, TLB

Revelation 12:11

16

Overcoming a Feeling of Rejection

Introduction

*R*ejection seems to create an identity crisis. Rejection by those in the Body of Christ is especially cruel, but it happens more often than it should. When you are thrown into an identity crisis, you have the opportunity to erase old tapes that have played in your mind for a long time, and replace those self-destructive thoughts with God-thoughts.

Your heavenly Father saw you and approved of you even while you were in your mother's womb. (Ps. 139:13-16.) He gave you survival tools that would bring you to the place where you are today. He is a Father Who has been waiting for you to come home to truth—the truth that will set you free. (John 8:32.)

Future rejection may hurt, but it will be only for a season. (1 Peter 1:6.) The Word of God is your shield against all the fiery darts of the devil. (Eph. 6:16,17.)

For victory over your feeling of rejection, pray the following prayer in faith and joy.[1]

Prayer

Lord, Your Son, Jesus, is my High Priest. He understands and sympathizes with my weaknesses and this excruciating pain of rejection. In His name I approach Your throne of grace with confidence, so that I may receive mercy and find grace to help me in my time of need. I ask You to forgive my sins, and I receive Your mercy; I expect Your healing grace to dispel the rejection I am suffering because of the false accusations and demeaning actions of another.

Father, Jesus was despised and rejected—a man of sorrows, acquainted with bitterest grief. The grief of _____'s turning against me and treating me as an outcast is consuming me, just as my rejection consumed Your Son, Who freely gave His life for me.

Forgive me for turning my back on Jesus and looking the other way—He was despised, and I didn't care. Yet it was my grief He bore, my sorrows that weighed Him down. He was wounded and bruised for my sins. He was

---

[1] For further support, I encourage you to read Psalm 27 and the book of Ephesians in their entirety.

beaten, that I might have peace; He was lashed, and with His stripes I was healed.

In the face of rejection I will declare, **The Lord is my Light and my Salvation—whom shall I fear or dread? The Lord is the Refuge and Stronghold of my life—of whom shall I be afraid?** (Ps. 27:1 AMP.)

I know right from wrong and cherish Your laws in my heart: I won't be afraid of people's scorn or their slanderous talk. Slanderous talk is temporal and fades away. Your Word will never pass away.

Father, I choose to look at the things that are eternal: Your justice and mercy shall last forever, and Your salvation from generation to generation. Your eyes are upon me, for I have right standing with You, and Your ears are attentive to my prayer. You spoke to me and asked, "Now who is going to hurt you if you are a zealous follower of that which is good?"

In my heart I set Christ apart as holy [and acknowledge Him] as Lord. I am always ready to give a logical defense to anyone who asks me to account for the hope that is in me, but I do it courteously and respectfully. I purpose [to see to it that] my conscience is entirely clear (unimpaired), so that when I am falsely accused as an evildoer, those who threaten me abusively and revile my right behavior in Christ may come to be ashamed [of slandering my good life].

There is wonderful joy ahead, even though the going is rough for a while down here. These trials are only to test my faith, to see whether it is strong and pure. It is being tested as fire tests gold and purifies it—and my faith is far more precious to You, Lord, than mere gold; so if my faith remains strong after being tried in the test tube of fiery trials, it will bring me much praise and glory and honor on the day of Jesus' return.

In spite of the rejection I have experienced, I declare that everything You say about me in Your Word is true:

> I am blessed with all spiritual blessings in heavenly places in Christ. (Eph. 1:3.)
>
> I am chosen by You, my Father. (Eph. 1:4.)
>
> I am holy and without blame. (Eph. 1:4.)
>
> I am Your child according to the good pleasure of Your will. (Eph. 1:5.)
>
> I am accepted in the Beloved. (Eph. 1:6.)
>
> I am redeemed through the blood of Jesus. (Eph. 1:7.)
>
> I am a person of wisdom and prudence. (Eph. 1:8.)
>
> I am an heir. (Eph. 1:11.)

I have a spirit of wisdom and revelation in the knowledge of Christ. (Eph. 1:17.)

I am saved by Your grace. (Eph. 2:5.)

I am seated in heavenly places in Christ Jesus. (Eph. 2:6.)

I am Your workmanship. (Eph. 2:10.)

I am near to You by the blood of Christ. (Eph. 2:13.)

I am a new creation. (Eph. 2:15.)

I am of Your household. (Eph. 2:19.)

I am a citizen of heaven. (Eph. 2:19.)

I am a partaker of Your promises in Christ. (2 Peter 1:4.)

I am strengthened with might by Your Spirit. (Eph. 3:16.)

I allow Christ to dwell in my heart by faith. (Eph. 3:17.)

I am rooted and grounded in love. (Eph. 3:17.)

I speak the truth in love. (Eph. 4:15.)

I am renewed in the spirit of my mind. (Eph. 4:23.)

I am Your follower. (Eph. 5:1.)

I walk in love. (Eph. 5:2.)

I am light in You. (Eph. 5:8.)

I walk circumspectly. (Eph. 5:15.)

I am filled with the Spirit. (Eph. 5:18.)

I am more than a conqueror. (Rom. 8:37.)

I am an overcomer. (Rev. 12:11.)

I am Your righteousness in Christ Jesus.
(1 Cor. 1:30.)

I am healed. (1 Peter 2:24.)

I am free. (John 8:36.)

I am salt. (Matt. 5:13.)

I am consecrated. (1 Cor. 6:11 AMP.)

I am sanctified. (1 Cor. 6:11.)

I am victorious. (1 John 5:4.)

Everything You say about me is true, Lord.

Scripture References

Hebrews 4:14-16 NIV   Isaiah 51:7,8 TLB

Isaiah 53:3-5 TLB   1 Peter 3:12-17 AMP

2 Corinthians 4:18   1 Peter 1:6,7 TLB

17

Overcoming Worry

*F*ather, I depart from evil and do good. I seek, inquire for and crave peace. I pursue (go after) it! When my ways please You, Lord, You make even my enemies to be at peace with me.

Lord, You have given to me Your peace; Your [own] peace You have bequeathed to me. It is not the peace that the world gives. I will not let my heart be troubled, neither will I let it be afraid. [I refuse to be agitated and disturbed; and I will not permit myself to be fearful and intimidated and cowardly and unsettled.]

Instead of worrying, I will pray. I will let petitions and praises shape my worries into prayers, letting You, Father, know my concerns, not forgetting to thank You for the answers. Your peace will keep my thoughts and my heart quiet and at rest as I trust in Christ Jesus, my Lord. It is wonderful what happens when Christ displaces worry at the center of my life.

Thank You for guarding me and keeping me in perfect and constant peace. My mind [both its inclination and its character] is stayed on You. I commit myself to You, lean on You and hope confidently in You.

I let the peace (soul harmony that comes) from Christ rule (act as umpire continually) in my heart [deciding and settling with finality all questions that arise in my mind]. I am thankful (appreciative), [giving praise to You always].

In Jesus' name, amen.

Scripture References

Psalm 34:14 AMP   Philippians 4:6,7 MESSAGE, TLB

Proverbs 16:7 AMP   Isaiah 26:3 AMP

John 14:27 AMP   Colossians 3:15 AMP

18

Overcoming Hypersensitivity

Introduction

"*A* new command I give you: Love one another. As I have loved you, so you must love one another. By this all men will know that you are my disciples, if you love one another."

John 13:34,35 NIV

The royal law of love is the counter-agent for hypersensitivity.

First Corinthians 13:5 AMP reveals that love **...is not conceited (arrogant and inflated with pride); it is not rude (unmannerly) and does not act unbecomingly. Love (God's love in us) does not insist on its own rights or its own way, for it is not self-seeking; it is not touchy or fretful or resentful; it takes no account of the evil done to it [it pays no attention to a suffered wrong].**

An overly sensitive person is thin-skinned and experiences feelings of alienation, irritability and resentment in relationships.

The hypersensitive person has usually experienced deep hurt from rejection and needs a lot of approval from others. This individual is excessively sensitive to remarks that may or may not be intended to be hurtful. It is difficult for a person of this nature to trust others, to accept constructive criticism or advice; and this weakness hinders positive relationships. When presentations or suggestions are rejected, that action is taken as a personal attack.

Hypersensitivity is an enemy that can be overcome through spiritual warfare. In waging the good warfare, we have God-given weapons to overthrow our adversary. These weapons include, among other things, the anointing that is upon Jesus to bind up and heal the brokenhearted (Luke 4:18), the Sword of the Spirit, which is the Word of God (Eph. 6:17), the shield of faith (Eph. 6:16), and the help of the Holy Spirit (John 14:16 AMP), which may come through a Christian counselor, a minister or a friend.

James instructed us, **Confess to one another therefore your faults (your slips, your false steps, your offenses, your sins) and pray [also] for one another, that you may be healed and restored [to a spiritual tone of mind and heart]. The earnest (heartfelt, continued) prayer of a righteous man makes tremendous power**

available [dynamic in its working] (James 5:16 AMP). We are overcomers by the blood of the Lamb and by the word of our testimony! (Rev. 12:11.)

Prayer

Father, forgive me for my attempts to hurt and dominate others. I realize that I have released my anger inappropriately. I confess this as sin and receive Your forgiveness, knowing that You are faithful and just to forgive my sin and cleanse me from all unrighteousness. I forgive those who have wronged me and ask for healing of my anger and unresolved hurts.

I realize that I am responsible for my own behavior, and I am accountable to You for my thoughts, words and actions.

Thank You for the Holy Spirit, Who leads me into reality—the truth, which makes me free. You have sent Your Word and healed me and delivered me from all my destructions.

Father, I am empowered through my union with You. I draw my strength from You [that strength which Your boundless might provides]. Your strength causes me to be steadfast and trustworthy, gives me the capacity for perseverance and tolerance and enables me to resist hypersensitivity, irritability and touchiness.

I desire to be well-balanced (temperate, sober of mind), vigilant and cautious at all times; for I recognize that enemy—the devil—who roams around like a lion roaring, seeking someone to seize upon and devour. In the name of Jesus, I withstand him, firm in faith [against his onset—rooted, established, strong, immovable and determined].

I am dwelling in the secret place of the Most High, and I shall remain stable and fixed under the shadow of the Almighty [Whose power no foe can withstand].

I purpose to walk in love toward my family members, my associates and my neighbors with the help of the Holy Spirit. Whom the Son has set free is free indeed.

Thanks be to You, Lord, for You always cause me to triumph in Christ Jesus. I am an overcomer by the blood of the Lamb and by the word of my testimony.

In Jesus' name, amen.

Scripture References

1 John 1:9	Ephesians 6:10 AMP
Mark 11:24,25	1 Peter 5:8,9 AMP
Matthew 12:36	Psalm 91:1 AMP
John 16:13	John 8:36
John 8:32	2 Corinthians 2:14
Psalm 107:20	Revelation 12:11

19

Overcoming Chronic Fatigue Syndrome

Introduction

*A*ll fatigue does not fall into the category of Chronic Fatigue Syndrome. Most people at one time or another have feelings of apathy and energy loss—times when they go to bed tired and get up tired.

There are cases of fatigue that last for weeks, months or even years. The medical profession has not determined the causes of Chronic Fatigue Syndrome and does not know its cure. In most individuals it simply runs its course.[1]

According to those who have shared with me their experience with this syndrome, they have flu-like symptoms—they feel achy with a low-grade fever. One person who suffers from it and for whom we pray is considered disabled and cannot work regularly.

---

[1] Editors of *Prevention Magazine,* "Symptoms, Their Causes & Cures" (Emmaus, PA: Rodale Press, 1994), pp. 179,181.

You and I are created triune beings—spirit, soul and body. (1 Thess. 5:23.) The Apostle John wrote, **Beloved, I wish above all things that thou mayest prosper and be in health, even as thy soul prospereth** (3 John 2).

God's Word is medicine to our flesh. (Prov. 4:20-22 AMP.) If any type of medication is to bring relief and a cure, it is necessary to follow the prescribed dosage. This is true with spiritual medicine as well. It is imperative to take doses of God's Word daily through reading, meditation and listening to healing tapes. The spirit, soul and body are interrelated; it is the Word of God that brings the entire being into harmony.

God made us and knows us inside and out. He sent His Word to heal us and to deliver us from all our destructions. (Ps. 107:20.) Prayer prepares us to take action. Jesus said that if we pray in secret, our heavenly Father will reward us openly. (Matt. 6:6.) Prayer includes praise, worship and petition.

Prayer prepares us for change—it equips us for action. It puts us in tune and in harmony with the Spirit of God, Who is hovering over the face of the rivers of living waters residing within us. (Gen. 1:2; John 7:38.) He is waiting for us to speak, to move—to act out our faith. The ministry of the Holy Spirit is revealed in the names ascribed to Him—Comforter, Counselor, Helper, Advocate,

Intercessor, Strengthener, Standby. (John 16:7 AMP.) He is with us and in us. (John 14:17.)

Prayer

Father, in the name of Jesus, I come before Your throne of grace to receive mercy and to find grace to help in time of need. May blessing (praise, laudation and eulogy) be to You, the God and Father of my Lord Jesus Christ (the Messiah), for You have blessed me in Christ with every spiritual (given by the Holy Spirit) blessing in the heavenly realm!

Father, Chronic Fatigue Syndrome is a curse, not a blessing. Jesus became a curse and at the same time dissolved the curse. And now, because of that, the air is cleared and I can see that Abraham's blessing is present and available for me. I am able to receive Your life, Your Spirit, just the way Abraham received it.

Christ, the Messiah, purchased my freedom with His very own blood, and the law of the Spirit of life [which is] in Christ Jesus [the law of my new being] has freed me from the law of sin and of death.

Christ lives in me. The Spirit of You Who raised up Jesus from the dead dwells in me. You, Father, are restoring to life my mortal (short-lived, perishable) body through Your Spirit, Who dwells in me.

You, Sovereign Lord, have given me an instructed tongue, to know the word that sustains the weary. You waken me morning by morning; You waken my ear to listen as one being taught.

I have strength for all things in Christ, Who empowers me [I am ready for anything and equal to anything through Him Who infuses inner strength into me; I am self-sufficient in Christ's sufficiency].

You are my Light and my Salvation—whom shall I fear or dread? You are the Refuge and Stronghold of my life—of whom shall I be afraid? You, Lord, are my Shield, my Glory and the Lifter of my head. With my voice I cry to You, and You hear and answer me out of Your holy hill. I lie down and sleep; I awaken again, and You sustain me.

Father, I put on Your whole armor; and, having done all, I stand, knowing that You are watching over Your Word to perform it. Your Word will not return to You void [without producing any effect, useless], but shall accomplish that which You please and purpose, and it shall prosper in the thing for which You sent it.

Lord, You used Your servant body to carry my sins to the cross so I could be rid of sin, free to live the right way. Your wounds became my healing.

I throw off the spirit of heaviness and exchange it for a garment of praise. Thank You for the superhuman energy that You so mightily enkindle and work within me.

In the name of Jesus I pray. Amen.

Scripture References

Hebrews 4:16	Psalm 3:3-5 AMP
Ephesians 1:3 AMP	Ephesians 6:11,13
Galatians 3:13,14 MESSAGE	Jeremiah 1:12 AMP
Acts 20:28	Isaiah 55:11 AMP
Romans 8:2,10,11 AMP	1 Peter 2:24 MESSAGE
Isaiah 50:4 NIV	Isaiah 61:3
Philippians 4:13 AMP	Colossians 1:29 AMP
Psalm 27:1 AMP	

20

Becoming Wise

I.

*F*ather, in the name of Jesus, I receive Your words and treasure up Your commandments within me. I make my ear attentive to skillful and godly wisdom. I incline and direct my heart and mind to understanding. I cry out for insight and raise my voice for understanding. I seek for wisdom as for silver, and I search for skillful and godly wisdom as for hidden treasures.

Then, I will understand the reverent and worshipful fear of You, Lord, and will find the knowledge of You—my omniscient God. Then, I will understand righteousness, justice and fair dealing [in every area and relation]; yes, I will understand every good path. For skillful and godly wisdom shall enter into my heart, and knowledge shall be pleasant to me. Discretion shall watch over me, and understanding shall keep me to deliver me from evil and from evil people.

In Jesus' name, amen.

Scripture References

Proverbs 2:1-5 AMP   *Proverbs 2:9-12* AMP

II.

Father, in all my ways, I acknowledge You, and You shall direct my paths.

You, Lord, by skillful and godly wisdom founded the earth; by understanding You established the heavens. It was in Christ that all things were created in heaven and on earth, things seen and things unseen, whether thrones, dominions, rulers or authorities; all things were created and exist through Him [by His service, intervention] and in and for Him.

In the name of Jesus, I keep sound and godly wisdom and discretion, and they are life to my inner self and a gracious ornament to my neck (my outer self). I walk in my way securely and in confident trust, that I shall not dash my foot or stumble. For You give Your angels [especial] charge over me to accompany and defend and preserve me in all my ways [of obedience and service]. They bear me up on their hands, lest I dash my foot against a stone.

Father, I walk uprightly; I walk securely, for I would not take a crooked way—then I would be found out and punished. When I lie down, I shall not be afraid; yes, I shall lie down, and my sleep shall be sweet. I am not afraid of sudden terror and panic, nor of the stormy blast or the storm and ruin of the wicked when it comes [for I will be guiltless]. In Christ I have my redemption through His blood.

You, Lord, are my confidence, firm and strong, and shall keep my foot from being caught [in a trap or some hidden danger].

Jesus is made unto me wisdom. Wisdom from You, Lord, makes prudence her dwelling and finds out knowledge and discretion. Because I have Your wisdom, I reverently fear and worship You, hating evil, pride, arrogance, the evil way and perverted and twisted speech. Your wisdom within me gives me counsel and sound knowledge, understanding and might and power.

I make it my quest in life to seek (aim at and strive after) first of all Your Kingdom and Your righteousness (Your way of doing and being right).

In the name of Jesus, amen.

Scripture References

Proverbs 3:6	Proverbs 3:24,25 AMP
Proverbs 3:19 AMP	Colossians 1:14 AMP
Colossians 1:16 AMP	Proverbs 3:26 AMP
Proverbs 3:21-23 AMP	1 Corinthians 1:30
Psalm 91:11,12 AMP	Proverbs 8:12-14 AMP
Proverbs 10:9 AMP	Matthew 6:33 AMP

21

Receiving a Discerning Heart

*F*ather, I thank You for creating within me a wise and discerning heart, so that I am able to distinguish between right and wrong.

This is my prayer: that my love may abound more and more in knowledge and depth of insight, so that I may be able to discern what is best and may be pure and blameless until the day of Christ, filled with the fruit of righteousness that comes through Jesus Christ—to Your glory and praise, O Lord.

Father, I trust in You with all my heart and lean not on my own understanding; in all my ways I acknowledge You, and You will make my paths straight. Through Your precepts I get understanding; therefore, I hate every false way. Your Word is a lamp to my feet and a light to my path.

Joseph in Genesis 41:39-41 NIV was described as a discerning and wise man who was put in charge of the entire land of Egypt. As You were with Joseph, so shall You be with me. You will cause me to find favor at my place of employment, at home or wherever I may be.

I make [special] request, [asking] that I may be filled with the full (deep and clear) knowledge of Your will in all spiritual wisdom and in understanding and discernment of spiritual things—that I may walk (live and conduct myself) in a manner worthy of You, Lord, fully pleasing to You and desiring to please You in all things, steadily growing and increasing in and by Your knowledge [with fuller, deeper and clearer insight, acquaintance and recognition].

Because Jesus has been made unto me wisdom, I listen and add to my learning; I discern and get guidance, understanding Your will.

In the name of Jesus, I pray. Amen.

Scripture References

1 Kings 3:9 NIV

Philippians 1:9-11 NIV

Proverbs 3:5 NIV

Psalm 119:104,105 AMP

Genesis 41:39-41 NIV

Joshua 1:5

Proverbs 3:1-4

Colossians 1:9,10 AMP

1 Corinthians 1:30

Proverbs 1:5

Ephesians 5:17

22

Developing Healthy Friendships[1]

*F*ather, help me to meet new friends—friends who will encourage me. May I find in these friendships the companionship and fellowship You have ordained for me. I know that You are my source of love, companionship and friendship. Your love and friendship are expressed through my relationship with You and members of the Body of Christ.

According to Proverbs 27:17 CEV, as iron sharpens iron, so friends sharpen the minds of each other. As we learn from each other, may we find a worthy purpose in our relationship. Keep me well-balanced in my friendships, so that I will always please You rather than pleasing other people.

I ask for divine connections—good friendships ordained by You. Thank You for the courage and grace to

---

[1] This prayer is composed of Scriptures and writings taken from "Meeting New Friends," *Prayers That Avail Much for Teens* (Tulsa: Harrison House, 1991), pp. 50-52.

let go of detrimental friendships. I ask and receive, by faith, discernment for developing healthy relationships. Your Word says that two are better than one, because if one falls, there will be someone to lift that person up.

Father, You know the hearts of people, so I won't be deceived by outward appearances. Bad friendships corrupt good morals. Thank You for quality friends who help me build a stronger character and draw me closer to You. Help me be a friend to others and to love my friends at all times. I will laugh with those who laugh, I will rejoice with those who rejoice and I will weep with those who weep. Teach me what I need to know to be a quality friend.

Develop in me a fun personality and a good sense of humor. Help me to relax around people and to be myself— the person You created me to be. Instruct my heart and mold my character, that I may be faithful and trustworthy over the friendships You are sending into my life.

Father, Your Son Jesus is my best Friend. He is a Friend Who sticks closer than a brother. He defined the standard when He said in John 15:13, **Greater love hath no man than this, that a man lay down his life for his friends.**

Thank You, Lord, that I can entrust myself and my need for friends into Your keeping. I submit to the leadership of the Holy Spirit, in the name of Jesus. Amen.

Scripture References

Proverbs 13:20 NIV	1 Corinthians 15:33 AMP
Ephesians 5:30 NIV	James 1:17 NIV
Philippians 2:2,3 NIV	Proverbs 17:17
Proverbs 13:20 NIV	Romans 12:15
Psalm 84:11 NIV	Proverbs 18:24
Ecclesiastes 4:9,10 NIV	Psalm 37:4,5 NIV

23

Maintaining Good Relations

*F*ather, in the name of Jesus, I will not withhold good from those to whom it is due [its rightful owners] when it is in the power of my hand to do it. I will render to all men their dues. I will [pay] taxes to whom taxes are due, revenue to whom revenue is due, respect to whom respect is due and honor to whom honor is due.

I will not lose heart and grow weary and faint in acting nobly and doing nobly and right, for in due season I shall reap if I do not loosen and relax my courage and faint. So then, as occasion and opportunity open up to me, I will do good [morally] to all people [not only being useful or profitable to them, but also doing what is for their spiritual good and advantage]. I am mindful to be a blessing, especially to those of the household of faith [those who belong to God's family with me, the believers].

I will not contend with a man for no reason—when he has done me no wrong. If possible, as far as it depends on me, I purpose to live at peace with everyone.

Scripture References

Proverbs 3:27 AMP	*Proverbs 3:30* AMP
Romans 13:7 AMP	*Romans 12:18* AMP
Galatians 6:9,10 AMP	

24

Improving Communication Skills

Introduction

*L*ack of communication skills is one of the greatest hindrances to healthy relationships. Most of the time when we pray, we are seeking change. We cannot change others, but we can submit to the constant ministry of transformation by the Holy Spirit. (Rom. 12:1,2.)

Prayer prepares us for change. Change produces change, which may be uncomfortable. If we will move through the discomfort, God will work with us, leading us out of our self-developed defense mechanisms into a place of victory. In this place He heals our brokenness and becomes our defense and our vindication. We are enabled to submit to the Champion of our salvation, which we are working out with fear and trembling. (Phil. 2:12.)

Adults who grew up in judgmental, critical homes where they were never allowed to express themselves sometimes carry much hurt and anger into their relationships.

Often, they were not permitted to have their own feelings without being condemned; they were not permitted to explore any ideas different than their parents' or caregivers'. There was an eye watching their every move. Any punishment they received was justified. Their parents were incapable of making a mistake.

Adult children of religiously rigid environments were led to believe that any slip, error in judgment or mistake was a sin that would send them straight to hell; the parents' religious doctrine was the only way to heaven and to deviate from it would lead to destruction. Forgiveness could be attained only after much sorrow, penance and retribution. Death before the completion of repentance led to an eternity in hell.

People raised in such oppressive home environments were never allowed to find themselves or to travel their own individual spiritual journeys leading to truth. The head of the home, usually the father, was God in the flesh. Conflict resolution was never taught or practiced. Whatever the head of the household said was law—and disobedience to his law was not discussed, but beaten out of the child. The wife was subservient and was not allowed to question the dictates of the husband.

When these adults marry, they often feel that they have finally found a platform from which to express themselves. They have escaped a place of abiding fear, constant condemnation and continual criticism. Having no communication skills, they often have difficulty expressing themselves properly. When anyone disagrees with them, they tend to react as they were taught. Only now, the marriage partner or friend does not submit to dogmatic, manipulative words. Frustration develops. The adult child seeks to make himself or herself understood, which results in more frustration. Anger is fed, and the individual continues to be in bondage to the idea that he or she should never have been born. The person either retreats to a silent corner, refusing to talk, or uses words to build walls of defense—shutting others out. He or she resides inside emotional isolation, attempting to remove himself or herself from more hurt and criticism.

There is a way of escape. God sent His Word to heal us and to deliver us from all our destructions. (Ps. 107:20.) We must determine to listen, to learn and to change with the help of the Holy Spirit—our Teacher, our Guide and our Intercessor. The anointing is upon Jesus to bind up and heal our emotional wounds. (Luke 4:18.) His anointing destroys every yoke of bondage (Isa. 10:27), setting the captives free.

Prayer

Father, I am Your child. Jesus said that if I pray to You in secret, You will reward me openly.

Father, I desire with all my heart to walk in love, but I am ever sabotaging my own efforts and failing in my relationships. I know that without faith it is impossible to please and be satisfactory to You. I am coming near to You, believing that You exist and that You are the rewarder of those who earnestly and diligently seek You.

Show "me" to me. Uncover me—bring everything to the light. When anything is exposed and reproved by the light, it is made visible and clear; and where everything is visible and clear there is light.

Heal the past wounds and hurts that have controlled my behavior and my speech. Teach me to guard my heart with all diligence, for out of it flow the very issues of life. Teach me to speak the truth in love in my home, in my church, with my friends and in all my relationships. Also, help me to realize that others have a right to express themselves. Help me to make room for their ideas, their opinions, even when they are different than mine.

Words are powerful. The power of life and death is in the tongue, and You said that I would eat the fruit of it.

Father, I realize that words can be creative or destructive. A word out of my mouth may seem of no account, but it can accomplish nearly anything—or destroy it! A careless or wrongly placed word out of my mouth can set off a forest fire. By my speech I can ruin the world, turn harmony to chaos, throw mud on a reputation, send the whole world up in smoke and go up in smoke with it—smoke right from the pit of hell. This is scary!

Father, forgive me for speaking curses. I am reacting out of past hurts and unresolved anger. At times I am dogmatic, even boasting that I am wise; sometimes, unknowingly I have twisted the truth to make myself sound wise; at times I have tried to look better than others or get the better of another; my words have contributed to things falling apart. My human anger is misdirected and works unrighteousness.

Father, forgive me. I cannot change myself, but I am willing to change and walk in the wisdom that is from above.

Father, I submit to that wisdom from above that begins with a holy life and is characterized by getting along with others. It is gentle and reasonable, overflowing with mercy and blessings, not hot one day and cold the next, not two-faced. Use me as Your instrument to develop a healthy, robust community that lives right with You. I will enjoy its results only if I do the hard work of getting along with others, treating them with dignity and honor.

With the help of the Holy Spirit and by Your grace, I will not let any unwholesome talk come out of my mouth, but only what is helpful for building others up according to their needs, that it may benefit those who listen.

My heart overflows with a goodly theme; I address my psalm to You, the King. My tongue is like the pen of a ready writer. Mercy and kindness shut out all hatred and selfishness, and truth shuts out all deliberate hypocrisy or falsehood; and I bind them about my neck, write them upon the tablet of my heart.

I speak excellent and princely things, and the opening of my lips shall be for right things. My mouth shall utter truth, and wrongdoing is detestable and loathsome to my lips. All the words of my mouth are righteous (upright and in right standing with You, Lord); there is nothing contrary to truth or crooked in them. My tongue is as choice silver, and my lips feed and guide many. I open my mouth in skillful and godly wisdom, and on my tongue is the law of kindness [giving counsel and instruction].

Father, thank You for loving me unconditionally. I thank You for sending Your Son, Jesus, to be my Friend and elder Brother and for giving me Your Holy Spirit to teach me and to bring all things to my remembrance. I am an overcomer by the blood of the Lamb and by the word of my testimony.

In the name of Jesus, I pray. Amen.

Scripture References

1 John 3:1	*Ephesians 4:29 NIV*
Matthew 6:6	*Psalm 45:1 AMP*
Hebrews 11:6 AMP	*Proverbs 3:3 AMP*
Ephesians 5:13 AMP	*Proverbs 8:6-8 AMP*
Proverbs 4:23	*Proverbs 10:20,21 AMP*
Ephesians 4:15	*Proverbs 31:26 AMP*
Proverbs 18:21	*Romans 8:31-39 NIV*
James 3:5,6 MESSAGE	*Hebrews 2:11 NIV*
James 3:9-16 MESSAGE	*John 15:15 NIV*
James 3:17	*John 14:26*
James 3:17,18 MESSAGE	*Revelation 12:11*

25

Selling Real Estate

*F*ather, I thank You for the skillful and godly wisdom needed in offering my house (or other real estate) to be sold. I am preparing my house (property) in excellence, that it may be beautiful and desirable as though I am preparing it for Your habitation. I am asking a fair and competitive market price and will not take advantage of a potential buyer.

Father, I ask that You prepare and send a *ready, willing* and *able* buyer to purchase my house (property). A person who has the funds available to pay the fair market value, pre-qualified and approved by a lending institution. One who has perfect timing of possession that fits into my need and his/hers.

Thank You for going before me and preparing the way. In the name of Jesus, I seek and pursue peace, thanking You that the Spirit of truth shall prevail in our deliberations. I declare and decree that everyone involved speaks truly, deals truly and lives truly.

Should there be anything that is hidden, I ask that it be revealed and brought to the light. Truth and mercy are written upon the tablets of my heart, and I have favor, good understanding and high esteem in Your sight and in the sight of the potential buyer.

In the name of Jesus, amen.

Scripture References

Proverbs 2:6,9,12,15 AMP   1 Corinthians 4:5 AMP

1 Corinthians 2:9   Proverbs 3:3,4 AMP

Ephesians 4:15 AMP

Needs and Concerns of the Single, Divorced and Widowed

Introduction

*T*he singles population has grown rapidly in the last decade. Single parent families are common. Some singles have never been married; some are recovering from the loss of their spouses through death or divorce.

Many singles are happily content with their status; however, many desire to be married. The prayers in this section were written in response to requests by singles and address their specific needs.

Single Again

The well-dressed young woman waited for the final amen before walking toward the exit. Her thoughts were jumbled with intense emotions. Silent screams hurt her throat, and churning tears threatened to run down her face.

Clutching her Bible and purse, Carol hoped that if she looked straight ahead, no one would speak to her. Walking briskly toward the parking lot, she saw couples holding hands. She heard the laughter of little children as they bounced along beside their doting parents. She had never felt more alone, and uninvited emotions were clamoring for release.

How could there be any more tears? She had allowed them to flow freely when she was alone. The nights were the worst—it seemed that daylight would never come. Finally, after six months, she acknowledged the reality of the divorce. There was nothing that could change it now. The reality was that her husband had remarried, and they were expecting the baby that should have been hers. She had made the decision to forgive them, but how long would it take to feel whole again?

Carol had looked forward to this day, feeling that it would be special. Upon awaking she felt vibrant and could hardly wait to get to church. Feeling a sense of expectancy in the air, she believed that this day would be her day of spiritual breakthrough. Instead, she felt let down, wondering where she belonged and how she would ever fit into a normal existence again.

Thoughts bouncing back and forth demanded to be heard as she walked. Since the divorce, she had continued going to church despite her growing discomfort. In the beginning, her friends were most supportive and rallied around her. Now, they appeared to feel uncomfortable when she approached. At times, they turned and walked away before she could speak to them. Why did she feel guilty when she reached out for a hug from men who had been like her brothers? They were stiff and withdrawn when their wives were present. Why were they fearful and suspicious of her motives? Did they no longer trust her? These were her friends who had vowed to be available when she needed them. Was this her imagination? She had grown up in this congregation—from childhood she felt that she belonged here. Why were her cherished relationships falling apart?

Usually very guarded in her thoughts, she allowed them to surface. What is the matter with me? What am I feeling? Instead of breakthrough, she felt distress. No longer able to fight the pain, she embraced it and asked the Holy Spirit to help her deal truly with herself, with Him and with others.

"Father, I don't understand what is happening to me." The gentle Voice spoke to her, "Carol, there is nothing wrong with you spiritually. You need emotional healing. I am the Healer and the Supplier of all your need. I am here to walk you through to victory."

Past scenes played in her head as she unlocked and opened the car door. Sliding behind the wheel of her car, she cried, "Help, God! How do I overcome these feelings that seem more powerful than me?"

Determining to take action, she reviewed her present circumstances. Yes, her life had changed drastically, not because she had chosen it, but because it had been chosen for her. It was time to take charge, make decisions and start rebuilding her personal life alone—without her husband. Maybe today was a breakthrough, but would the pain ever go away?

"Lord," she prayed, "reveal me to *me*. Help me see myself as you see me. Show me where I have missed the mark, and give me the grace to trust You and myself. I submit to the ministry of constant transformation by the Holy Spirit. I can't change myself—I don't even know what needs changing. You have planned paths in which I am to walk. Teach me to live; teach me to pray."

The Support Group

Carol entered the room in the annex building of the church and was astonished to see so many seats filled. As she looked around, she recognized many faces—some she knew personally, others she had never seen. The group facilitator opened the meeting with a short prayer, welcoming the Holy Spirit, declaring his dependence on Him and asking for His leadership.

The support group of both men and women was very quiet and nervously awaited instructions. Prayer time had felt so safe. Now all eyes were on the man who began explaining the evening's agenda. Carol realized that they were being asked to introduce themselves and state their reasons for coming.

The young man seated next to her introduced himself and said that he wanted to learn to control his temper in hopes that he could be reunited with his family.

A single mother gave her name, sharing the frustration of being deserted by the father of their three children. She briefly spoke of how difficult her financial situation had become—living from payday to payday, hoping the children wouldn't get sick or need additional school supplies. A scholarship had been provided by a friend; otherwise she could not have signed up for the support group. She didn't know why she had come, except to please her friend. Others were not sure why they had come either.

Carol listened as, one by one, each expressed a personal need or reason for coming. She felt chagrined when it came her turn to speak. Compared to most of these people, her life seemed blessed, her problems relatively few and minor.

Then she remembered that though their circumstances might be different, pain is pain. She was here to work on herself, to discover how she had contributed to the breakup of her marriage, to find herself and improve her relationship with God. Her trust level was low, but she knew that she needed help to recover from the shock of the divorce. Coming here to ask for help, to seek support, was one of the most humiliating, most humbling experiences of her life. She had always considered herself self-sufficient.

As she was driving home, she rehearsed the things she had heard from different individuals. She had not given much thought to remarrying, for she did not consider herself single. But, *The fact is,* she realized, *I am single in the eyes of the world. How does God look at me now?*

She reflected on the statements of one man: "The fear that I will never marry consumes me, opens the door to temptation and hinders my spiritual growth. Then, the fear is turned inward—something must be dreadfully wrong with me.

"I am tired of sinning, repenting, sinning, repenting and promising God that I will never commit the sin again—only to find myself in another compromising situation. It has occurred to me that I help create these situations."

Over the coming few months, some members of the group fell away. Those remaining received insight into the plan of God. Confessing their sins to God and to each other, they repented. With each confession there arose new hope, strength and courage. At times they wept with one another. When someone experienced emotional healing and spiritual growth, they rejoiced.

The water of the Word was cleansing them, washing away the thoughts and attitudes that exalted themselves above the knowledge of God. They encouraged one another as their minds were being renewed to the Word.

The group members validated one another, listened without judging and were not surprised as Carol's leadership abilities emerged. The facilitator guided their discussions and directed them again and again to the Bible for clarification and wisdom.

Single and Complete

Carol sensed an intense urging to read God's Word. Her reading in the past had been mechanical, formed by years of training. Now, the Word seemed to leap off the pages and was emblazoned on the tablets of her heart. She could not read enough or fast enough. Aware of the presence of God, Carol was growing more intimately acquainted with Him as He communicated with her. She came alive to the Word, and God's Word was alive in her.

At this point, Carol returned to the support group to share her newly inspired meditations and understandings that had developed in her life. Transformation was taking place, and her desires were changing—her desire to know God intensified. For years she had done all the "right" things required of her by others. Now, she wanted to please God, to do His will and to be used of Him. Scriptures that she had heard all her life were profound and meaningful. God's Word was spirit and life to her!

Each week she returned to the support group—listening, sharing and listening. The Holy Spirit began to reveal areas of her life that were distasteful. Self-righteous? "Oh, God, forgive me and change me." Scornful of others? "Oh, God, forgive me. Wash me, and I shall be whiter than snow." Selfish, self-centered? "Oh, God, forgive me. Thank You, Father, for the Holy Spirit, Who is at work in me. Forgive me and cleanse me from the sin of pride. I am here, Lord. All to Jesus I surrender. Use me as Your instrument to help others."

Prayer, fellowship with God, became her way of life. She met with her pastor to share the vision of a prayer group for singles. The group would be established on James 5:16 AMP. **Confess to one another therefore your faults (your slips, your false steps, your offenses, your sins) and pray [also] for one another, that you may be healed and restored [to a spiritual tone of mind and heart]. The earnest (heartfelt, continued) prayers of a righteous man make tremendous power avail [dynamic in its working].** The Bible would be their prayer manual.

On the final evening the remaining members met at her home for refreshments. Carol shared her vision of a prayer group and invited everyone to participate. Carol's excitement inspired the mother of three, and she expressed an interest in attending. She no longer saw herself as a victim and was moving into a place of victory in Jesus, learning to trust Him more.

The young man who had been so desperate to get married had resolved personal issues and received healing for his crippled emotions. He realized that God was his Source, and he was ready to move on in God.

Others expressed changes in their views of life and recognized a need to know God more intimately. The facilitator looked on with tears in his eyes, thankful for the working of the Holy Spirit in the group. Not every group was as receptive to spiritual transformation and emotional wholeness. He was thankful for Carol's obedience and influence on the group to hear God and was excited to know that most would be attending the prayer group. He had done all that he could for this group, and his thoughts were already moving ahead to the next group, who would be meeting in a few weeks. In the meantime he would be praying and seeking God's direction and guidance.

26

Abiding in Jesus

Introduction

*L*et no one say when he is tempted, I am tempted from God; for God is incapable of being tempted by [what is] evil and He Himself tempts no one.

But every person is tempted when he is drawn away, enticed and baited by his own evil desire (lust, passions).

Then the evil desire, when it has conceived, gives birth to sin, and sin, when it is fully matured, brings forth death.

James 1:13-15 AMP

Single people sometimes express the difficulty of keeping themselves pure. (See the following prayers on purity.) Some have asked, "Doesn't God understand that we are only human? Why did He create us with desires; surely He understands and excuses us when we fall into temptation? If He wants me to avoid sexual temptation, then why doesn't He send me the spouse I have asked Him to give me?"

The Scriptures condemn premarital sex, fornication, adultery and all forms of sexual perversion. (Matt. 15:19; Mark 7:21 AMP; Gal. 5:19-21; Col. 3:5,6.) Although sexual desires are not a sin, if not properly controlled, those desires can lead to sin.

According to James 1:13-15, sin begins with a thought conceived from lust. Lust is not limited to sex. It is possible to lust after many things that can cause sin. That's why it is so important to take control over the mind and heart—to keep them pure and holy in spite of temptation.

One of the myths that has ensnared many single people is the mistaken idea that marriage will automatically release them from the temptation to sin. Without repentance and the renewing of the mind, those who have a problem with lustful thoughts before they are married will have the same problem after they are married, just as those who have a problem with sexual perversion before marriage will continue to have the same problem after marriage.

One married man shared his testimony of deliverance from pornography. He was having to continually guard himself from mental images that kept reappearing.

Marriage is not a cure-all for sexual sins or any other sin.

Yes, God does understand. With every temptation He has provided a way of escape. (1 Cor. 10:13.)

Yes, there is forgiveness for sin (1 John 1:9)—through God's abounding grace. (Rom. 5:20.) The question is **...Are we to remain in sin in order that God's grace (favor and mercy) may multiply and overflow? Certainly not! How can we who died to sin live in it any longer?** (Rom. 6:1,2 AMP.)

We who are in Christ desire to bring glory to the Father. We cannot do so in our own strength. It is abiding in union with Jesus and loving as Jesus loves that ensures answered prayer. (John 15:7-9.) If our prayers are not being answered, it is time to check our love walk. We must ask ourselves, "Are we keeping ourselves in the love of God—remaining vitally united with Jesus?"

> **We know [absolutely] that anyone born of God does not [deliberately and knowingly] practice committing sin, but the One Who was begotten of God carefully watches over and protects him [Christ's divine presence within him preserves him against the evil], and the wicked one does not lay hold (get a grip) on him or touch [him].**
>
> **1 John 5:18** AMP

This verse says that the wicked one cannot touch us. What is the condition? Having Christ's presence within, staying united with Him—abiding in Him and allowing His Word to abide in us.

If you want to abide in Christ and have His Word abide in you, pray the following prayer with a sincere and believing heart.

Prayer

Lord, I am abiding in Your Word [holding fast to Your teachings and living in accordance with them]. It is my desire to be Your true disciple. I am abiding in (vitally united to) the vine. I cannot bear fruit unless I abide in You.

Lord, because You are the Vine and I am a branch living in You, I bear much (abundant) fruit. Apart from You [cut off from vital union with You] I can do nothing. Your Son, Jesus, said, **If you live in Me [abide vitally united to Me] and My words remain in you and continue to live in your hearts, ask whatever you will, and it shall be done for you** (John 15:7 AMP).

When I bear (produce) much fruit, You Father, are honored and glorified. By Your grace, which I have received, I will show and prove myself to be a true follower of Your

Son, Jesus. He has loved me, [just] as You, Father, have loved Him. I am abiding in that love.

Lord, You have assured me that if I keep Your commandments [if I continue to obey Your instructions], I will abide in Your love and live on in it, just as Your Son, Jesus, obeyed Your commandments and lived on in Your love. He told me these things, that Your joy and delight may be in me and that my joy and gladness may be of full measure and complete and overflowing. This is Your commandment: that we love one another [just] as You have loved us.

Father, thank You for Your Word—it is the truth that makes me free. I am born (begotten) of You, Lord, and I do not [deliberately, knowingly and habitually] practice sin. Your nature abides in me [Your principle of life, the divine sperm, remains permanently within me]; and I cannot practice sinning, because I am born (begotten) of You. I have hidden Your Word in my heart, that I might not sin against You.

May Christ through my faith [actually] dwell (settle down, abide, make His permanent home) in my heart! It is my desire to be rooted deep in love and founded securely on love, that I may have the power and be strong to apprehend and grasp with all the saints [Your devoted people, the experience of that love] what is the breadth and length and height and depth [of it].

I pray, in the name of Jesus, that I may know this love that surpasses knowledge—that I may be filled to the measure of all Your fullness. Now to You Who are able to do immeasurably more than all I ask or imagine, according to Your power that is at work within me, to You be glory in the Church and in Christ Jesus throughout all generations, forever and ever! Amen.

Scripture References

John 8:31 AMP	*1 John 3:9* AMP
John 15:4,5 AMP	*Psalm 119:11*
John 15:7-12 AMP	*Ephesians 3:17,18* AMP
John 8:32	*Ephesians 3:19-21* NIV
John 17:17	

27

Knowing God's Plan for Marriage

*U*nto You, O Lord, do I bring my life. O my God, I trust in, lean on, rely on and am confident in You. Let me not be put to shame or [my hope in You] be disappointed; let not my enemies (rejection, hurt, inferiority, unworthiness) triumph over me.

Father, it is written, **For I know the thoughts and plans that I have for you, says the Lord, thoughts and plans for welfare and peace and not for evil, to give you hope in your final outcome. Then you will call upon Me, and you will come and pray to Me, and I will hear and heed you. Then you will seek Me, inquire for, and require Me [as a vital necessity] and find Me when you search for Me with all your heart. I will be found by you, says the Lord...** (Jer. 29:11-14 AMP).

In the name of Jesus, I always pray and do not turn coward (faint, lose heart and give up).

Father, I am looking for Your plan, Your answer for my life. It is my desire to be married. But, I must be sure in my decision that I am living as You intend and accepting whatever situation You have put me into. According to Your Word, marriage will bring extra problems that I may not need to face at this time in my life.

All the ways of a man or woman are pure in his or her own eyes, but You, Lord weigh the spirits (the thoughts and intents of the heart). Therefore, I roll my works upon You, [commit and trust them wholly to You; You will cause my thoughts to become agreeable to Your will, and] so shall my plans be established and succeed.

Because You, Lord, are my Shepherd, I have everything I need!

You let me rest in the meadow grass and lead me beside the quiet streams. You give me new strength. You help me do what honors You the most.

Even when walking through the dark valley of death I will not be afraid, for You are close beside me, guarding, guiding me all the way.

You provide delicious food for me in the presence of my enemies. You have welcomed me as Your guest; my blessings overflow!

Your goodness and unfailing kindness shall be with me all of my life, and afterwards I will live with You forever in Your home.

In Jesus' name I pray, amen.

Scripture References

Psalm 25:1,2 AMP	*Proverbs 16:2,3 AMP*
Luke 18:1 AMP	*Psalm 23:1-6 TLB*
1 Corinthians 7:1,2 TLB	

28

Finding a Mate

Introduction

*I*n our ministry we hear from many men and women who desire to be married. If that is your desire, we encourage you to ask the Lord to prepare you for marriage. Submit to God's future plans for your life, and purpose to please Him. Do not make your deliberations without knowing His will, at the expense of your personal spiritual growth and transformation. Going from glory to glory (2 Cor. 3:18) is not dependent on having a spouse.

Most of the time, each partner brings a lot of emotional baggage into the marriage relationship. As you prepare for marriage, remember that the anointing that was upon Jesus (Luke 4:18,19) is within you. This anointing will destroy every yoke of bondage (Isa. 10:27) as God exposes emotional wounds and heals your brokenness.

Knowing the reality of your completeness in Christ Jesus will enable you to enter into a healthy relationship, one in which both you and your partner will grow together spiritually and in every other area of life. Seeking first the

Kingdom of God and His righteousness (Matt. 6:33), doing those things that are pleasing in His sight (1 John 3:22), will prepare you to be the person designed by Him to fulfill the role of husband or wife.

This prayer is written for your own growth and benefit.

Prayer

Father, I come before You in the name of Jesus, asking for Your will to be done in my life as I look to You for a marriage partner. I submit to the constant ministry of transformation by the Holy Spirit, making my petition known to You.

Prepare me for marriage by bringing everything to light that has been hidden—wounded emotions, walls of denial, emotional isolation, silence or excessive talking, anger or rigidity *[name any wall that separates you from healthy relationships and God's love and grace]*. The weapons of my warfare are not carnal, but mighty through You, Lord, to the pulling down of strongholds.

I know the One in Whom I have placed my confidence, and I am perfectly certain that the work, whether I remain unmarried or marry, is safe in Your hands until that day.

Because I love You, Lord, and because I am called according to Your plan, everything that happens to me fits into a pattern for good. In Your foreknowledge, You chose me to bear the family likeness of Your Son. You chose me long ago; when the time came You called me; You made me righteous in Your sight and then lifted me to the splendor of life as Your child.

Since I am surrounded by such a great cloud of witnesses, let me throw off everything that hinders and the sin that so easily entangles, and let me run with perseverance the race marked out for me. Let me fix my eyes on Jesus, the author and perfecter of my faith, Who for the joy set before Him endured the cross, scorning its shame, and sat down at the right hand of Your throne, O God. I consider Him Who endured such opposition from sinful men, so that I will not grow weary and lose heart.

I turn my back on the turbulent desires of youth and give my positive attention to goodness, integrity, love and peace in company with all those who approach You, Lord, in sincerity. I have nothing to do with silly and ill-informed controversies, which lead inevitably to strife. As Your servant, I am not a person of strife. I seek to be kind to all, ready and able to teach. I seek to be tolerant and have the ability to gently correct those who oppose Your message.

Father, I desire and earnestly seek (aim at and strive after) first of all Your Kingdom and Your righteousness (Your way of doing and being right), and then all these things taken together will be given me besides. So I do not worry and will not be anxious about tomorrow.

I am persuaded that I can trust You because You first loved me. You chose me in Christ before the foundation of the world. In Him the whole fullness of Deity (the Godhead) continues to dwell in bodily form [giving complete expression of the divine nature]; and I am in Him, made full and have come to the fullness of life [in Christ].

I am filled with the Godhead—Father, Son and Holy Spirit—and I reach toward full spiritual stature. And He (Christ) is the Head of all rule and authority [of every angelic principality and power]. So, because of Jesus, I am complete; Jesus is my Lord.

I come before You, Father, expressing my desire for a Christian mate. I petition that Your will be done in my life. Now I enter into that blessed rest by adhering to, trusting in and relying on You.

In Jesus' name, amen.

Scripture References

Matthew 6:10	*Matthew 6:33,34* AMP
1 Corinthians 4:5	*1 John 4:19*
2 Corinthians 10:4	*Ephesians 1:4*
2 Timothy 1:12 PHILLIPS	*Colossians 2:9,10* AMP
Romans 8:28-30 PHILLIPS	*Matthew 6:10*
Hebrews 12:1-3 NIV	*Hebrews 4:10*
2 Timothy 2:22-25 PHILLIPS	*John 14:1* AMP

29

Developing Patience

*F*ather, I come before You in the name of Jesus. I desire to meditate, consider and inquire in Your presence. Waiting patiently for a marriage partner has become a challenge— a trial, sometimes leading to temptation. I am asking for Your help in developing patience, quietly entrusting my future to Your will. It is to You that I submit my desire to be married.

By Your grace I surrender my life—all my desires, all that I am and all that I am not—to the control of the Holy Spirit Who produces this kind of fruit in me: love, joy, peace, *patience,* kindness, goodness, faithfulness, gentleness and self-control; and here there is no conflict. I belong to Jesus Christ and seek to live by the Holy Spirit's power and follow the Holy Spirit's leading in every part of my life. [In exercising] self-control I [develop] steadfastness (patience, endurance), and in [exercising] steadfastness I [develop] godliness (piety).

By faith, I consider it wholly joyful whenever I am enveloped in, or encounter, trials of any sort or fall into various temptations. It is then that I am reminded to rest assured and understand that the trial and proving of my faith brings out endurance and steadfastness and patience. I purpose to let endurance and steadfastness and patience have full play and do a thorough work, so that I may be perfectly and fully developed [with no defects], lacking in nothing.

Father, fill me with the knowledge of Your will through all spiritual wisdom and understanding, that I may live a life worthy of You and may please You in every way: bearing fruit in every good work, growing in the knowledge of You, being strengthened with all power according to Your glorious might so that I may have great endurance and patience and joyfully giving thanks to You Who have qualified me to share in the inheritance of the saints in the Kingdom of light.

Father, I strip off and throw aside every encumbrance (unnecessary weight) and that sin which so readily (deftly and cleverly) clings to and entangles me, and I run with patient endurance and steady and active persistence the appointed course of the race that is set before me. I look away [from all that will distract] to Jesus, Who is the Leader and the Source of my faith [giving the first incentive for my belief] and is also its Finisher [bringing it to maturity and perfection].

With patience I am able to persevere through the difficult times—times of anxiety and worry—and overcome the fear that I may never be married. I am an overcomer by the blood of the Lamb and by the word of my testimony.

In Jesus' name, amen.

Scripture References

Psalm 3:4 AMP   James 1:2-4 AMP

Psalm 37:4,5   Colossians 1:9-12 NIV

Galatians 5:22-25 TLB   Hebrews 12:1,2 AMP

2 Peter 1:6 AMP   Revelation 12:11

30

Preparing Self for Marriage

*F*ather, sometimes being single can be so lonely, so painful. Seeing people in pairs, laughing and having fun, makes me feel even more alone and different.

Lord, please comfort me in these times. Help me to deal with my feelings and thoughts in an appropriate way. Help me to remember to work hard on myself, so that I will be whole and mature when You bring the right person into my life.

Help me to remember that this is a time of preparation for the day when I will be joined to another human being for life. Show me how to be responsible for myself and how to allow others to be responsible for themselves.

Teach me about boundaries—what they are and how to establish them instead of walls. Teach me about love—Your love—and how to speak the truth in love as Jesus did.

Father, I don't want to be a hindrance to my future spouse, to You or to myself. Help me to take a good look at myself, at my self-image. Lead me to people—teachers, preachers, counselors—and to things—books, tapes, seminars—anyone and anything You can use to teach me Your ways of being and doing right and being whole.

Teach me how to choose the mate You would have for me. Give me the wisdom I need to see clearly and not to be double-minded. Help me to recognize the qualities You would have me look for in a mate.

Father, thank You for revealing to me that the choice of a mate is not to be based only on emotions and feelings, but that You have very definite guidelines in the Bible for me to use. I know that when I put these principles into practice, I will save myself a lot of pain and trouble.

Thank You that You are not trying to make things hard for me, but that You know me better than I know myself. You know my situation—You know the beginning from the end. You know the qualities and attributes that are needed in another person that will make me happy in our shared life together and will make that person happy with me.

I pray that you will keep my foot from being caught in a hidden trap of danger. I cast the care of this decision on You, knowing that You will cause my thoughts to come in line with Your will so that my plans will be established and succeed.

In Jesus' name I pray, amen.

Scripture References

1 Corinthians 1:3,4 NIV	James 1:5-8
Ephesians 4:15	Proverbs 3:26 AMP
Matthew 6:33 AMP	Proverbs 16:3 AMP

31

Committing to a Life of Purity

*F*ather, I come before Your throne of grace in the name of Jesus. At one time I walked [habitually], following the course and fashion of this world [under the sway of the tendency of this present age]. I lived and conducted myself in the passions of my flesh [my behavior governed by my corrupt and sensual nature], obeying the impulses of the flesh and the thoughts of my mind [my cravings dictated by my senses and my dark imaginings].

But God, You are so rich in Your mercy! Even when I was dead (slain) by [my own] shortcomings and trespasses, You made me alive together in union with Christ, and it is by Your grace (Your favor and mercy that I did not deserve) that I am saved (delivered from judgment and made a partaker of Christ's salvation). You raised me up together with Him and made us sit down together [giving me joint seating with Him] in the heavenly sphere in Christ Jesus (the Messiah, the Anointed One).

You are my Father; I am Your child. Since I am in Christ, I am a new creature; old things have passed away; and, behold, all things have become new.

In accordance with Your Word, I rid myself of all malice and all deceit, hypocrisy, envy and slander of every kind. Like a newborn baby, I crave pure spiritual milk so that by it I may grow up in my salvation now that I have tasted that You, Lord, are good.

Father, forgive me for the years of watching, reading and listening to vile things. I submit to Jesus Christ, Who loves me and gave Himself up for me, so that He might sanctify me, having cleansed me by the washing of water with the Word, that He might present me to Himself in glorious splendor, without spot or wrinkle or any such things [that I might be holy and faultless].

Thank You for the blood of Christ, Who through the eternal Spirit offered Himself unblemished to You, which cleanses my conscience from acts that lead to death, so that I may serve You, the living God! Thank You for the Holy Spirit, Who indwells me. He is holy (chaste, pure).

I ask for and receive an impartation of the wisdom that comes from heaven—it is first of all pure; then peace-loving, considerate, submissive, full of mercy and good fruit, impartial and sincere.

May my words issue from a pure heart, and may they be pleasing to You.

Lord, Your Holy Spirit is my Counselor—[change my impure language] and give to me a clear and pure speech from pure lips, that I may call upon Your name, to serve You.

I am transformed (changed) by the [entire] renewal of my mind, and I bring my thoughts into obedience to Your Word. I fix my thoughts on what is true and good and right. I determine to think about things that are pure and lovely, and dwell on the fine, good things in others. I think about all I can praise You for, and I am glad. I keep and guard my heart with all vigilance and, above all, that I guard, for out of it flow the springs of life.

What [an incredible] quality of love You have given (shown, bestowed upon) me, that I should [be permitted to] be named and called and counted a child of God! I am [even here and] now Your child; it is not yet disclosed (made clear) what I shall be [hereafter], but I know that when Jesus comes and is manifested, I shall [as Your child] resemble and be like Him, for I shall see Him just as He [really] is. I have this hope [resting] on Him, and I cleanse (purify) myself just as He is pure (chaste, undefiled, guiltless).

Through the power of the Holy Spirit given to me, I am an overcomer by the blood of the Lamb and by the word of my testimony!

In Jesus' name I pray, amen.

Scripture References

Ephesians 2:2-6 AMP	Proverbs 15:16 AMP
2 Corinthians 5:17	Zephaniah 3:9 AMP
1 Peter 2:1,2 NIV	Romans 12:2 AMP
Psalm 101:3 NIV	2 Corinthians 10:5
Ephesians 5:25-27 AMP	Philippians 4:8 TLB
Hebrews 9:14 NIV	Proverbs 4:23 AMP
1 Thessalonians 4:8 AMP	1 John 3:1-3 AMP
James 3:17 NIV	Revelation 12:11

I.

A Man of Purity

Father, I attend to Your Word. I hide it in my heart, that I might not sin against You. It is not wrong to have sexual desires. You made me, You know me and You bought me. I belong to You. I commit myself and all my natural affections to You, Father, and acknowledge the power of the Holy Spirit in my life. I give Him control and submit to Your will.

Forgive my former sins against You, against myself and against others. Thank You for Your grace, which enables me to leave my gift at the altar when I remember that someone has a grievance against me. I will go and make peace with that person whenever possible and then come back and present my gift to You.

In the name of Jesus, I thank You for the power to shun immorality and all sexual looseness. I [flee from impurity in thought, word or deed]. My body is the temple (the very sanctuary) of the Holy Spirit, Who lives within me, Whom I have received [as a gift] from You. I am not my own. I was bought with a price [purchased with a preciousness and paid for, made Your own]. So then, I will honor You, Father, and bring glory to You in my body.

When I read Your Word, I receive the truth that makes me free. I have won my battle with Satan. I have learned to know You as my Father. I am strong with Your Word in my heart. I no longer love this evil world and all that it offers me, for when I love these things I show that I do not really love You, Lord; for all these worldly things, these evil desires—the craze for sex, the ambition to buy everything that appeals to me and the pride that comes from wealth and importance—are not from You, Father.

They are from this evil world itself. This world is fading away, and these evil, forbidden things will go with it; but whoever keeps doing Your will, Lord, will live forever.

Thank You, Father, that I have been anointed by [I hold a sacred appointment from, and I have been given an unction from] the Holy One, and I know [the truth]. I have received the Holy Spirit, and He lives within me, in my heart, so that I don't need anyone to teach me what is right. For He teaches me all things, and He is the Truth and no liar; and so, just as He has said, I must live in Christ, never to depart from Him.

O Father, I stay in happy fellowship with You, so that when Your Son, Jesus, comes I will be sure that all is well and will not have to be ashamed and shrink back from meeting Him. I know that You are always good and do only right, and I seek to be an imitator of You and do what is good and right.

In Jesus' name, amen.

Scripture References

Proverbs 4:20	*1 John 2:12-17 TLB*
Psalm 119:11	*1 John 2:20,27-29 TLB*
Matthew 5:23,24 AMP	*Matthew 6:33 AMP*
1 Corinthians 6:18-20 AMP	*Ephesians 5:1 AMP*
John 8:32 AMP	

II.

A Woman of Purity

Father, on the authority of Your Word I declare and decree that I am a new creation in Christ. I repent of my former sins, receive Your forgiveness and renew my mind—replacing old thought patterns and habits with Your thoughts and plans for me.

I was a sinner, separated (living apart) from Christ. But now in Christ Jesus, my Lord, I have been brought near through the blood of Christ. I confess that Jesus is my Lord and believe in my heart that You raised Him from the dead. Therefore, I am engrafted in Christ (the Messiah). Now, today, I am a new creation (a new creature altogether); the old [previous moral and spiritual condition] has passed away. Behold, the fresh and new has come!

Since I have confidence to enter the Most Holy Place by the blood of Jesus, by a new and living way opened for me through the curtain, that is, His body, and since I have a great Priest over the house of God, I draw near to You, Lord, with a sincere heart in full assurance of faith, having my heart sprinkled to cleanse me from a guilty conscience and having my body washed with pure water. I hold unswervingly to the hope I profess, for He Who promised is faithful. And I consider how I may spur others on toward love and good deeds. I will not give up meeting together, as some are in the habit of doing; but I will encourage others, and all the more as I see the day approaching.

Father, I am Your daughter (Your handmaiden), and You have poured out Your Spirit upon me, and I shall prophesy [telling forth the divine counsels and predicting future events pertaining especially to Your Kingdom]. I seek (aim at and strive after) first of all Your Kingdom and Your righteousness (Your way of doing and being right), and then all these things taken together will be given me besides. I will not worry or be anxious about tomorrow, for tomorrow will have worries and anxieties of its own. Sufficient for each day is its own trouble.

As Your daughter, I thank You for enduing me with Your grace (free, spontaneous, absolute favor and loving-kindness). With You, Father, nothing is ever impossible, and no word from You shall be without power or impossible of fulfillment.

Father, I submit to Your will for my life. Your ways are higher than my ways, Your thoughts higher than my thoughts. I commit my way to You, and You will cause my thoughts to become agreeable to Your will, and so shall my plans be established and succeed. I am Your handmaid; let it be done to me according to Your Word.

Since I have such a huge crowd of men and women of faith watching me from the grandstands, I strip off anything that slows me down or holds me back, and especially those sins that wrap themselves so tightly around my feet and trip me up; and I run with patience the particular race that You have set before me. I keep my eyes on Jesus, my Leader and Instructor.

Father, to the pure You show Yourself pure, and to the willful You show Yourself willful. The afflicted people You will deliver, but Your eyes are upon the haughty, whom You will bring down. For You, O Lord, are my Lamp; You, Lord lighten my darkness. For by You I run through a troop; by You I leap over a wall. As for You, Lord, Your way is perfect; Your Word is tried. You are my Shield, for I trust and take refuge in You.

O Father, that I might ascend the hill of the Lord and stand in Your Holy Place. I come with clean hands and a pure heart, refusing to lift up my soul to an idol or swear by what is false, that I may receive blessing and vindication from You, my God and my Savior. Surely, Lord God, You are good to those who are pure in heart.

In Jesus' name I pray, amen.

Scripture References

2 Corinthians 5:17

Romans 12:1,2 AMP

Jeremiah 29:11 AMP

Ephesians 2:12,13 AMP

Romans 10:9

2 Corinthians 5:17 AMP

Hebrews 10:19-25 NIV

Acts 2:17 AMP

Matthew 6:33,34 AMP

Luke 1:28,30,37 AMP

Isaiah 55:9 AMP

Proverbs 16:3 AMP

Luke 1:38 AMP

Hebrews 12:1,2 TLB

2 Samuel 22:27-31 AMP

Psalm 24:3-5 NIV

Psalm 73:1 NIV

32

Letting Go of Bitterness

Introduction

*I*n interviews with divorced men and women, I have been encouraged to write a prayer on overcoming bitterness.

Often, the injustice of the situation in which these people find themselves creates deep hurts, wounds in the spirit and anger that is so near the surface that the individuals involved risk sinking into the trap of bitterness and revenge. Their thoughts may turn inward as they consider the unfairness of the situation and dwell on how badly they have been treated.

In a family divorce situation, bitterness sometimes distorts ideas of what is best for the child/children involved. One parent (and sometimes both parents) will use the child/children against the other.

Unresolved anger often moves one marriage partner to hurt the one he or she holds responsible for the hurt and sense of betrayal he or she feels.

There is healing available. There is a way of escape for all who will turn to the Healer, obeying Him and trusting Him.

Prayer

Father, life seems so unjust, so unfair. The pain of rejection is almost more than I can bear. My past relationships have ended in strife, anger, rejection and separation.

Lord, help me to let go of all bitterness and indignation and wrath (passion, rage, bad temper) and resentment (anger, animosity).

You are the One Who binds up and heals the brokenhearted. I receive Your anointing, which destroys every yoke of bondage. I receive emotional healing by faith, and I thank You for giving me the grace to stand firm until the process is complete.

Thank You for wise counselors. I acknowledge the Holy Spirit as my wonderful Counselor. Thank You for helping me work out my salvation with fear and trembling, for it is You, Father, Who work in me to will and to act according to Your good purpose.

In the name of Jesus, I choose to forgive those who have wronged me. I purpose to live a life of forgiveness because You have forgiven me. With the help of the Holy Spirit, I get rid of all bitterness, rage, anger, brawling and slander, along with every form of malice. I desire to be kind and compassionate to others, forgiving them, just as in Christ You forgave me.

With the help of the Holy Spirit, I make every effort to live in peace with all men and to be holy, for I know that without holiness no one will see You, Lord. I purpose to see to it that I do not miss Your grace and that no bitter root grows up within me to cause trouble and defile me.

I will watch and pray that I enter not into temptation or cause others to stumble.

Thank You, Father, that You watch over Your Word to perform it and that whom the Son has set free is free indeed. I declare that I have overcome resentment and bitterness by the blood of the Lamb and by the word of my testimony.

In Jesus' name, amen.

Scripture References

Ephesians 4:31 AMP	*Ephesians 4:31,32 NIV*
Luke 4:18	*Hebrews 12:14,15 NIV*
Isaiah 10:27	*Matthew 26:41*
Proverbs 11:14	*Romans 14:21*
John 15:26 AMP	*Jeremiah 1:12 AMP*
Philippians 2:12,13 NIV	*John 8:36*
Matthew 5:44	*Revelation 12:11*

Needs and Concerns of Marriage Partners and Heads of Households

33

Blessing the Household

Introduction

*A*s the head of the family, it is your privilege and duty to pray for the household in your charge and those under your care and authority.

The following prayer was written to be prayed by a man or a woman. So often, in today's society, the woman finds herself having to assume the responsibility and position of the head of the household.

I.

Prayer of Blessing for the Household

Father, as the priest and head of this household, I declare and decree, "As for me and my house, we shall serve the Lord."

Praise be to You, the God and Father of our Lord Jesus Christ, for You have blessed us in the heavenly realms with every spiritual blessing in Christ. We reverence You and worship You in spirit and in truth.

Lord, we acknowledge and welcome the presence of Your Holy Spirit here in our home. We thank You, Father, that Your Son, Jesus, is here with us because we are gathered together in His name.

Lord God, Your divine power has given us everything we need for life and godliness through our knowledge of You, Who called us by Your own glory and goodness.

As spiritual leader of this home, I declare on the authority of Your Word that my family will be mighty in the land; this generation of the upright will be blessed.

Father, You delight in the prosperity of Your people; and we thank You that wealth and riches are in our house and our righteousness endures forever.

In the name of Jesus, amen.

Scripture References

Revelation 1:6	2 Peter 1:3 NIV
Joshua 24:15	Psalm 112:2 NIV
Ephesians 1:3 NIV	Psalm 25:37
John 4:23	Psalm 112:3
Matthew 18:20	

II.

Prayer of Blessing at the Table

Introduction

This prayer was written for the head of the household to pray not only to thank and praise God for His blessings, but also to cleanse and consecrate the food received and to sanctify the family members who partake of it.

Prayer

Father, thank You for giving to us our daily bread. We receive this food with thanksgiving and praise. You bless our bread and our water and take sickness out of the midst of us.

In the name of Jesus, we call this food clean, wholesome and pure nourishment to our bodies. Should there be any deadly thing herein, it shall not harm us, for the Spirit of life in Christ Jesus makes us free from the law of sin and death.

In the name of Jesus, amen.

Scripture References

Matthew 6:11   Mark 16:18

1 Timothy 4:4 NIV   Romans 8:2

Exodus 23:25

III.

Husband's Prayer of Blessing for His Wife

Introduction

It is positive reinforcement, validation and affirmation for children to hear their father pray, blessing his wife and their mother. This is a method of honoring her and reaffirming her position in the home. Words are powerful, and the blessings for the wife in front of the children will promote appropriate self-esteem necessary for success in life.

Sometimes, a wife will feel that she has failed because she is not fulfilling all the roles expressed in Proverbs 31. I believe that God had this passage written to encourage a woman to be all that He created her to be. Out of her "being"—knowing herself (both her strengths and her weaknesses), developing her talents, seeing herself as God sees her and looking to Christ for her completeness (wholeness)—comes the "doing."

"The woman described in this chapter has outstanding abilities. Her family's social position is high. In fact, she may not be one woman at all—she may be a composite portrait of ideal womanhood. Do not see her as a model to imitate in every detail; your days are not long enough to do everything she does! See her instead as an inspiration to be all you can be. We can't be just like her, but we can learn from her industry, integrity and resourcefulness."[1]

Prayer

Father, I thank You for my wife, who is a capable, intelligent and virtuous woman. Her worth is far more precious than jewels, and her value is far above rubies or pearls.

I thank You that she is a woman of strong character, great wisdom, many skills and great compassion. Strength and dignity are her clothing, and her position is strong and secure. She opens her mouth with skillful and godly wisdom, and on her tongue is the law of kindness [giving counsel and instruction].

---

[1] *Life Application Bible*, New International Version edition (Wheaton, IL: Tyndale House Publishers, 1988, 1989, 1990, 1991), commentary at bottom of p. 1131.

Our children rise up and call her blessed (happy, fortunate and to be envied); and I boast of and praise her, [saying], "Many daughters have done virtuously, nobly and well [with the strength of character that is steadfast in goodness], but you excel them all."

Father, my wife reverently and worshipfully fears You; she shall be praised! Give her of the fruit of her hands, and let her own works praise her in the gates [of the city].

I respect, value and honor my wife before our children.

In the name of Jesus. Amen.

Scripture References (AMP)

Proverbs 31:10	*Proverbs 31:28,29*
Proverbs 31:25,26	*Proverbs 31:30,31*

IV.

Parent's Prayer of Blessing for Children

Introduction

"The [Hebrew] father's place in the [traditional Jewish] home is fittingly shown by the beautiful custom of blessing the children, a custom which dates back to Isaac and Jacob. To this day, in many homes, the father blesses his children on Friday nights, on Rosh Hashanah eve and on Yom Kippur before leaving for the synagogue....

"In very ancient times, the father or patriarch was the ruler of home and family. He made laws and enforced them. Later, however, laws were instituted by teachers, parents, judges and kings. The father, as the master of the house, was looked up to for support and depended on for guidance."[2]

The following prayer, based on a translation of the traditional Hebrew father's blessing upon his children, may be used by the head of the household, whether male or female.

Prayer

Father, I receive, welcome and acknowledge each of my children as a delightful blessing from You. I speak Your blessings upon them and over them.

Children, I bless you in the name of Jesus, proclaiming the blessings of God, my Redeemer, upon you. May He give you wisdom, a reverential fear of God and a heart of love.

---

[2] Ben M. Edidin, *Jewish Customs and Ceremonies* (New York: Hebrew Publishing Company, 1941), p. 23.

May He create in you the desire to attend to His words, a willing and obedient heart that you may consent and submit to His sayings and walk in His ways. May your eyes look straight ahead with purpose for the future. May your tongue be as the pen of a ready writer, writing mercy and kindness upon the tablets of your heart. May you speak the truth in love. May your hands do the works of the Father; may your feet walk the paths He has foreordained for you.

I have no greater joy than this—to hear that my children are living their lives in the truth.

May the Lord prepare you and your future mate to love and honor one another, and may He grant to your union upright sons and daughters who will live in accordance with His Word. May your source of livelihood be honorable and secure, so that you will earn a living with your own hands. May you always worship God in spirit and in truth.

I pray above all things that you may always prosper and be in health even as your soul prospers. **...I know the thoughts and plans that I have for you, says the Lord, thoughts and plans for welfare and peace and not for evil, to give you hope in your final outcome** (Jer. 29:11 AMP).

In the name of Jesus. Amen.

Scripture References

Psalm 127:3 AMP	Ephesians 2:10 AMP
Philippians 2:13 AMP	3 John 4 AMP
Proverbs 4:20	1 Thessalonians 4:11,12 NIV
Psalm 45:1	John 4:23
Proverbs 3:3 AMP	3 John 2
Ephesians 4:15	

34

Handling Household Finances

Introduction

*T*he following prayers may be prayed individually or as a couple. In preparation for marriage it is great wisdom for the couple to discuss finances. Each party comes with an individual view of how to handle money—spending and/or saving. It is wise to set up a budget that is agreeable to both.

There is a danger in the tendency to assume that the other party has the same opinions and ideas about money or, in case of disagreement, that one's own way is right and the other person's is wrong. Financial differences is one of Satan's greatest weapons for introducing strife and bringing pressure to bear on a marriage. Spending money can quickly evolve into an emotional experience, causing many other problems.

God is *El-Shaddai*, God Almighty (Ex. 6:3 AMP)— the God Who is more than enough—and His intention is that His children enjoy good health and that all may go well with them, even as their souls are getting along well.

(3 John 2 NIV.) Two people coming into agreement with God's financial plan will offset the enemy's schemes to divide and conquer.

If you and your beloved are planning to marry or to establish a financial plan in your existing marriage, listen to one another. Understand what each other is saying. Realize that there are differences in viewpoints about money and allow for those differences. Determine who is more astute in financial matters: balancing the checkbook, paying the bills on time and making wise investments. Set aside time in your schedules to keep each other informed, review goals and make plans. Wisdom from above is willing to yield to reason; cooperate one with the other. (James 3:17 AMP.)

Prayer

Father, we come before You in the name of Jesus. Thank You for the Holy Spirit, Who is present with us as we discuss our financial future together. We thank You for bringing us to this place in our lives. You have started a good work in us and will perform it until the day of Christ. We welcome You as we prepare to set up a budget that is pleasing to You and to each of us.

Jesus is our Lord and our High Priest, and we purpose to bring Him the firstfruits of our income and worship You, the Lord our God, with them.

Father, You are Lord over our marriage—over this union that we believe has been ordained by You. We confess Your Word over our life together and our finances. As we do so, we say that Your Word will not return to You void, but will accomplish what it says it will do.

Therefore, we believe in the name of Jesus that all our needs are met, according to Your riches in glory. We acknowledge You as Lord over our finances by giving tithes and offerings to further Your cause.

Father, on the authority of Your Word we declare that gifts will be given to us; good measure, pressed down, shaken together and running over shall they be poured into our bosom. For with the same measure we deal out, it shall be measured back to us.

We remember that it is written in Your Word that he who sows sparingly and grudgingly will also reap sparingly and grudgingly, and he who sows generously [that blessings may come to someone] will also reap generously and with blessings.

Lord, remind us always, and we purpose to remember, that it is You Who give us power to become rich, and You do it to fulfill Your promise to our ancestors. We will never feel that it was our own power and might that made us wealthy.

Father, not only do we give tithes and offerings to You, but we also give to those around us who are in need.

Your Word also says that he who gives to the poor lends to You and You pay wonderful interest on the loan! We acknowledge You as we give for the benefit of the poor.

Thank You, Father, that as You bless us and we bless others, they will praise You and give You thanks and bless others and the circle of Your love and blessing will go on and on into eternity.

In the name of Jesus we pray. Amen.

Scripture References

John 14:17	Luke 6:38
Philippians 1:6	2 Corinthians 9:6 AMP
Hebrews 3:1	Deuteronomy 8:17,18 TLB
Deuteronomy 26:10,11	Proverbs 19:17 TLB
Isaiah 55:11	2 Corinthians 9:12-15 AMP,
Philippians 4:19	NIV, PHILLIPS

I.

Setting Aside the Tithe

Father, Your Word states, **Be sure to set aside a tenth of all that your fields produce each year....so that you may learn to revere the Lord Your God always**

(Deut. 14:22,23 NIV). We purpose to set aside the tithe because it belongs to You, O God our Father.

It is our delight to bring all the tithes (the whole tenth of our income) into the storehouse, that there may be food in Your house. Lord of hosts, in accordance with Your Word, we prove You now by paying You the tithe. You are opening the windows of heaven for us and pouring us out a blessing, that there shall not be room enough to receive it.

Thank You, Father, for rebuking the devourer for our sakes; he shall not destroy the fruits of our ground, neither shall our vine drop its fruit before the time in the field.

We praise You, Lord, for recording our names in Your book of remembrance of those who reverence and worshipfully fear You and who think on Your name so that we may be Yours in the day when You publicly recognize and openly declare us to be Your jewels (Your special possession, Your peculiar treasure).

Thank You for bringing us out of the authority of darkness and translating us into the Kingdom of Your dear Son, Jesus Christ, our Lord.

In His name we pray, amen.

Scripture References

Malachi 3:10,11 AMP   *Colossians 1:13*

Malachi 3:16,17 AMP

II.
Giving the Offering

Father, we give offerings at the direction of the Holy Spirit. We are ever ready with a generous and willing gift. At Your instructions we remember this: He who sows sparingly and grudgingly will also reap sparingly and grudgingly, and he who sows generously [that blessings may come to someone] will also reap generously and with blessings.

We [give] as we make up our own minds and purpose in our hearts, not reluctantly or sorrowfully or under compulsion; for You, Lord, love (take pleasure in, prize above other things and are unwilling to abandon or to do without) a cheerful (joyous "prompt to do it") giver [whose heart is in his giving].

Father, we thank You that You are able to make all grace (every favor and earthly blessing) come to us in abundance, so that we may always and under all circumstances and whatever the need be self-sufficient [possessing enough to require no aid or support and furnished in abundance for every good work and charitable donation].

Father, [You] provide seed for our sowing and bread for our eating. Thank You for providing and multiplying [our resources], for sowing and increasing the fruits of our righteousness. Thus we will be enriched in all things and in every way, so that we can be generous, and [our generosity as it is] administered by us will bring forth thanksgiving to You.

We confess with the psalmist David, we have not seen the righteous forsaken, nor his seed begging bread.

We thank You for food, clothing and shelter. In the name of Jesus, we determine to stop being perpetually uneasy (anxious and worried) about our life together, what we shall eat and what we shall drink, or about our bodies, what we shall put on. Our life—individually and together— is greater [in quality] than food, and our bodies [far above and more excellent] than clothing.

The bread of idleness [gossip, discontent and self-pity] we will not eat. We declare on the authority of Your Word that our family will be mighty in the land: This generation of the upright will be blessed.

Father, You delight in the prosperity of Your people; and we thank You that wealth and riches are in our house and that our righteousness endures forever.

Good comes to us, for we are generous and lend freely and conduct our affairs with justice. When we lack wisdom, we will ask of You, and You will give generously without finding fault with us.

In the name of Jesus, amen.

Scripture References

2 Corinthians 9:5-11 AMP   Psalm 112:2,3

Psalm 37:25   Psalm 37:26 NIV

Matthew 6:25 AMP   2 Corinthians 9:9 AMP

Proverbs 31:27 AMP   James 1:5 NIV

Psalm 35:27

35

Adopting a Child

*F*ather, in Jesus' name, we come boldly before Your throne of grace, that we may receive mercy and find grace to help in our time of need. We are trusting in You and seek to do good; so that we may dwell in the land and feed surely on Your faithfulness.

We delight ourselves also in You, and You give us the desires and secret petitions of our hearts. We believe our desire to adopt a child is from You, and we are willing to assume the responsibility of rearing this child in the ways of the Master.

Father, we commit our way to You [roll and repose each care of our load on You]. Our confidence is in You, and You will bring this adoption to pass according to Your purpose and plan.

Lord, Your Son, Jesus, demonstrated Your love for children when He said, **"...Let the children alone, don't prevent them from coming to me. God's kingdom is made up of people like these"** (Matt. 19:14 MESSAGE). Then, He laid hands on them and blessed them.

Use us as Your instruments of peace and righteousness to bless this child. We purpose in our hearts to train this child up in the way that he/she should go.

Lord, we are embracing this child (Your best gift) as our very own with Your love, as Jesus said, **"Whoever embraces one of these children as I do embraces me, and far more than me—God who sent me"** (Mark 9:37 MESSAGE).

Father, take this child up and be a Father and Mother to him/her as we extend our hands and our hearts to embrace him/her. Thank You for the blood of Jesus that gives protection to this one whom we love.

We thank You for the man and woman who conceived this child and pray that You will bless them, cause Your face to shine upon them and be merciful to them. If they do not know Jesus, we ask You, the Lord of the harvest, to send forth laborers to share truth with them, that they may come out of the snare of the devil.

Mercy and truth are written upon the tablets of our hearts, and You cause us to find favor and good understanding with You and with man—the adoption agency staff, the judges and all those who are involved in this decision-making process. May all be careful that they do not despise one of these little ones over whom they have jurisdiction—for they have angels who see Your face continually in heaven.

We believe that all our words are righteous (upright and in right standing with You, Father). By our long forbearing and calmness of spirit those in authority are persuaded, and our soft speech breaks down the most bone-like resistance.

Lord, we are looking to You as our Great Counselor and Mighty Advocate. We ask for Your wisdom for us and our attorneys.

Father, contend with those who contend with us, and give safety to our child and ease him/her day by day. We are calling on You in the name of Jesus, and You will answer us and show us great and mighty things. No weapon formed against us and this adoption shall prosper, and any tongue that rises against us in judgment we shall show to be in the wrong. This [peace, righteousness, security and triumph over opposition] is our inheritance as Your children.

Father, we believe; therefore, we have spoken. May it be done unto us according to Your Word.

In Jesus' name, amen.

Scripture References

Hebrews 4:16

Psalm 37:3

Psalm 37:4 AMP

Ephesians 6:4 MESSAGE

Psalm 37:5 AMP

Proverbs 22:6

Psalm 67:1

Matthew 9:38

2 Timothy 2:26

Proverbs 3:3,4

Matthew 18:10 PHILLIPS

Proverbs 8:8 AMP

Proverbs 25:15 AMP

James 1:5

Isaiah 49:25

Jeremiah 33:3

Isaiah 54:17 AMP

Psalm 116:10

Luke 1:38

36

Moving to a New Location

*F*ather, Your Word says that You will perfect that which concerns us. Your mercy and loving-kindness, O Lord, endure forever—forsake not the works of Your own hands. We bring to You our apprehensions concerning our relocation. We ask You to go before us to make the crooked places straight in finding a new home.

Give us wisdom to make wise decisions in choosing the movers and packers best suited to handle our possessions. We have favor, good understanding and high esteem in the sight of You and man—with the utility companies, with the school systems and with the banks—with everyone involved in this move.

Father, we thank You for supplying and preparing the new friends that You would want us to have. We are trusting You to direct us to a church where we can fellowship with like believers, in one accord, where we are free to worship and praise You and sing to You a new song.

Father, in the name of Jesus, we commit this move to You, knowing that You provide for Your children. We trust

You and delight ourselves in You, and You will give us the desires of our hearts.

We make all these requests known unto You with thanksgiving, and the peace that passes all understanding shall guard our hearts and minds. You will keep us in perfect peace because our minds are stayed on You.

We trust in You, Father, with all our hearts. We lean not unto our own understanding; but in all our ways we acknowledge You, and You shall direct our paths.

Thank You, Father, for Your blessing on this move.

In the name of Jesus. Amen.

Scripture References

Psalm 138:8	Psalm 40:3
Isaiah 45:2	Psalm 96:1
James 1:5	Psalm 98:1
Proverbs 3:4	Psalm 149:1
Hebrews 10:25	Psalm 37:4,5
Acts 2:1,46	Philippians 4:6,7
Acts 4:34	Isaiah 26:3
Philippians 2:2	Proverbs 3:5,6
Isaiah 42:10	

37

Seeking Safety in a Place of Violence

*F*ather, I am Your child. I have been redeemed by the blood of the Lamb. My sins are forgiven.

As the head of my household, I pray according to Your Word, asking for Your protection for each of us. Give safety to my children and ease them day by day. Our life is exceedingly filled with the scorning and scoffing of those who are at ease and with the contempt of the proud (irresponsible tyrants who disregard Your law).

Lord, You see the violence that is in the streets and in our schools. The drug dealers, the gang members living in our neighborhoods are waiting to snare our children.

On the authority of Your Word, I ask that You destroy [their schemes]; O Lord, confuse their tongues, for I have seen violence and strife in the inner city. Day and night they go about on its walls; iniquity and mischief are in its midst. Violence and ruin are within it; fraud and guile do not depart from its streets and marketplaces. I am calling upon You, Lord, and You will save me and my household as well.

Father, in the name of Jesus, You and You alone are our safety and our protection. My household and I are looking to You, for our strength comes from You—the God Who made heaven and earth. You will not let us stumble. You are our Guardian God Who will not fall asleep. You are right at our side to protect us. You guard us from every evil, You guard our very lives. You guard us when we leave and when we return. You guard us now; You guard us always.

My household was chosen and foreknown by You, Father, and consecrated (sanctified, made holy) by the Spirit to be obedient to Jesus Christ (the Messiah) and to be sprinkled with [His] blood. We receive grace (spiritual blessing) and peace in ever increasing abundance [that spiritual peace to be realized in and through Christ, freedom from fears, agitating passions and moral conflicts].

Lord, Your Son, Jesus, became our Passover by shedding His own precious blood. He is the Mediator (the Go-between, Agent) of a new covenant, and His sprinkled blood speaks of mercy. On the authority of Your Word, I proclaim that the blood of Jesus is our protection, as it is written, **...when I see the blood, I will pass over you...** (Ex. 12:13). I declare and decree that I am drawing a blood-line around my children, and the evil one cannot cross it.

I know that none of the God-begotten make a practice of sin—fatal sin. The God-begotten are also the God-protected. The evil one can't lay a hand on my household. I know that we are held firm by You, Lord.

Father, thank You for Your divine protection. In the name of Jesus, I pray. Amen.[1]

Scripture References

1 John 3:1	Psalm 121:1-8 MESSAGE
1 Peter 1:18,19	1 Peter 1:2 AMP
1 John 2:12	Hebrews 12:24 AMP
Psalm 123:4 AMP	1 John 5:18,19 MESSAGE
Psalm 55:9-11,16 AMP	

---

[1] In addition to praying this prayer, read Psalm 91 aloud over your family each day.

38

Dealing With an Abusive Family Situation

Introduction

*I*n our ministry, we receive letters from women who are living in abusive situations. Since many of them do not feel or believe that they can leave, they request that we write prayers to cover this area of need. They are fearful of practicing tough love. A need for security plays a big role in their decision to remain where they are. Or, in certain cases they fear increased or even more severe abuse should they try to leave. Others have asked the abuser to leave or have moved out themselves; yet, their request is for prayer for deliverance for the abuser and other family members.

When I am traveling, I often meet women who feel that it is safe to talk with me. At the close of a meeting a few years ago, I was approached by an attractive woman whom I recognized by her manner of dress as belonging to a certain denomination. As she shared her agony and emotional pain, I moaned inwardly. I took her in my arms, encouraging her to go to her pastor for counseling. Her answer grieved me. She had been told by both her husband and her pastor that the beatings were because of her "rebellious nature."

"I don't know what else I can do to stop the abuse," she confided. "I've tried to please my husband. Scripturally, I cannot leave him. What can I do but stay with him? I don't want to disobey God, but I want the abuse to stop."

When we turn to the Scriptures, we find that God is much more merciful than we human beings. Jesus is our Example, and in one incident He turned around and walked away from the crowd who would have thrown Him off a cliff. (Luke 4:28-30.) There are times to take action; change brings change. Often, we want God to do something when all the time He is waiting for us to do something: **Trust God from the bottom of your heart; don't try to figure out everything on your own. Listen for God's voice in everything you do, everywhere you go; he's the one who will keep you on track** (Prov. 3:5,6 MESSAGE).

A testimony of deliverance from abusive behavior was shared by a young husband who had been born again for only a short time. His mother had given him a copy of *The Living Bible*. One day he picked it up and read Malachi 2:15,16: **You were united to your wife by the Lord. In God's wise plan, when you married, the two of you became one person in his sight. And what does he**

want? Godly children from your union. Therefore guard your passions! Keep faith with the wife of your youth. For the Lord, the God of Israel, says he hates divorce and cruel men. Therefore control your passions—let there be no divorcing of your wives.

The young man said, "When I read these verses, I realized that I was treating my wife cruelly and admitted to myself that the addictions in my life were controlling me. It wasn't so much that I wanted to stop doing drugs, but I did want to change the way that I was treating my wife. I cried out to God, and He heard me and delivered me."

The following prayer was written for Christian women who want to know how to pray prayers that avail much while in an abusive family situation.

Prayer

Father, Your Word says that You loved me and my family so much that You sent Your very own Son, Jesus, to die for our sin so we could live with You forever. You said that You would give us a new life that is wonderful and rich. I pray that I may become like You, for I am Your child and You love me.

By Your grace, Father, I will live my life in love. Your love in me is not a feeling, but a decision requiring more than mere words. As a Christian I am "light," and I will live as a child of the light. The light produces in me all that is good and right and true.

Lord, lead me in paths of righteousness for Your name's sake. I purpose to live, with a due sense of responsibility, not as others who do not know the meaning of life but as one who does. Direct me by Your Holy Spirit, that I may make the best use of my time, despite all the evils of these days.

Father, there was a time that You looked for an intercessor. I am willing to stand in the gap and make up the hedge so that my family will not suffer judgment. Send Your Holy Spirit to convict, convince and demonstrate to us about sin, righteousness and judgment. Give us a heart of flesh and send a laborer of the harvest to share with us the Gospel of the glory of Christ (the Messiah).

I thank You, Father, that each family member who is lost receives and confesses that Jesus is his/her Lord, and I ask that Your will be done in his/her life. It is You Who rescue him/her from the dominion of darkness, and You translate him/her into the Kingdom of the Son of Your love. In the name of Jesus, I ask that You help him/her to grow in grace, that he/she may experience Your love and trust You to be his/her Father.

Lord, reveal the steps that I should take to break what appears to be a generational curse. The sins of the fathers are being repeated in our household, and I do not want this curse passed down to my children.

Father, Your Word says that we are overcomers by the blood of the Lamb and by the word of our testimony. In the name of Jesus, I am committing my life to You—to obey You. Show me the path of life for me and my family.

Uncontrollable, irrational anger, rage and abuse are a curse. Your Son, Jesus, was made a curse for us; therefore, I put on Your whole armor, that I may be able to successfully stand against all the strategies and the deceits of the devil.

In the name of Jesus, I am the redeemed, and I plead the blood of Jesus over my family. I thank You that the evil power of abuse is broken, overthrown and cast down out of my family. The abuse is exposed and reproved by the light; it is made visible and clear, and where everything is visible and clear there is light.

You sent Jesus to bind up our heartaches and to heal our pain. The Bible says that You have sent Your Word to heal us and to deliver us from our own destructions. Give us the grace and faith to receive healing and to forgive those who have abused us; and thank You for the courage to make amends to those whom we have harmed.

Teach us how to guard our hearts with all diligence. I declare and decree that we are growing in grace and the knowledge of You, developing the trust we need to receive Your transforming power to change. I make my petitions known to You with thanksgiving, in the name of Jesus. Amen.

Scripture References

John 3:16	1 Peter 3:18
John 10:10	Revelation 12:11
Ephesians 5:1 PHILLIPS	Psalm 16:11
1 John 3:18 AMP	Galatians 3:13
Ephesians 5:8,9 PHILLIPS	Ephesians 6:11 AMP
Psalm 23:3	Ephesians 5:13 AMP
Ephesians 5:15,16 PHILLIPS	Luke 4:18
Ezekiel 22:30	Psalm 107:20
John 16:8 AMP	Matthew 5:44
Ezekiel 11:19	Proverbs 4:23
Matthew 9:38	Romans 12:2
Matthew 6:10	Philippians 4:6 NIV
Colossians 1:13	

39

Overcoming Weariness

*T*his prayer is for everyone who is experiencing weariness. It is not limited to the unmarried who are awaiting a life-partner. Many spouses become weary with heartaches that they did not expect to encounter in marriage. Their expected marriage bliss has turned into disappointment, additional wounds and frustration. They are weary with waiting for the healing of the marriage relationship or the deliverance of a spouse, children or other loved ones from various addictions or negative, destructive behaviors. They long for someone who will heal their wounds without judging them—someone who will love them unconditionally.

Each individual brings baggage into marriage, hoping for a miracle—each partner looking to the other for acceptance and approval.

According to the letters and comments we have received in our ministry, unmarried people experience weariness in matters that married couples may not encounter. Hopefully, we who are married share respon-sibilities—household chores. Married homeowners may divide the work up into inside and outside labor. Sometimes, one spouse neglects his/her responsibility, and the other finds himself/herself doing the work of two. The single person is responsible at all times for "the work of two."

We who are married have another individual involved in the decision-making process, which can lead to conflict. Conflict is not always bad. Out of this conflict can come intimacy. We are not alone in financial decisions, in planning for the future. We may feel alone, but there is another with whom we can talk, with whom we can explore possibilities. We have another human being from whom we can draw strength. Ideally, we grow together.

Sometimes, a married person may experience feelings of "aloneness," but there is another person in the house, someone who is going to return, someone whose presence—although in certain marriages non-communicative—is experienced.

The unmarried often feel such weariness and dread going home to emptiness—to nothingness. They look for that individual who will be their soul-mate, a life partner, someone who will be present and available in good times and bad, someone who will love them unconditionally.

(We must all ask ourselves, "Am I ready and willing to love another person unconditionally?")

If you have grown weary and are disappointed in your expectations, I encourage you to seek God for His plan for your life. Ask the Holy Spirit to help you trust God and not be afraid.

Prayer

Father, You see my weariness, my uneasiness proceeding from continual waiting and disappointed expectation. It seems that my patience is exhausted, and I am discouraged. I am weary of asking and waiting for _____.

My soul is weary with sorrow; strengthen me according to Your Word.

Lord, I come to you, and You give me rest. I take Your yoke upon me and learn of You, for You are gentle and humble in heart, and I will find rest for my soul. Your yoke is easy, and Your burden is light.

I look to You, Lord, and Your strength; I seek Your face always. You are my Refuge and Strength, an ever-present help in trouble. O my Strength, I watch for You; You, O God, are my Fortress, my loving God. O my Strength, I sing praise to You.

Father, You give strength to the weary and increase the power of the weak. Even youths grow tired and weary, and young men stumble and fall; but those who hope in You, Lord, will renew their strength. They will soar on wings like eagles; they will run and not grow weary. They will walk and not be faint. I purpose to wait for You, Lord; to be strong and take heart and wait for You.

Lord, You are my Strength and my Song; You have become my Salvation. You are my God, and I will praise You, my father's God, and I will exalt You. In Your unfailing love You will lead the people You have redeemed. In Your strength You will guide them to Your holy dwelling.

You, Sovereign Lord, have given me an instructed tongue, to know the word that sustains the weary. You waken me morning by morning, waken my ear to listen like one being taught.

You are my Light and my Salvation—whom shall I fear or dread? You are the Refuge and Stronghold of my life—of whom shall I be afraid? You are a shield for me, my Glory, and the Lifter of my head. With my voice I cry to You, Lord, and You hear and answer me out of Your holy hill. Lord, You sustain me.

I consider it wholly joyful whenever I am enveloped in or encounter trials of any sort or fall into various temptations. I am assured and understand that the trial and proving of my faith bring out endurance and steadfastness and patience. I purpose to let endurance and steadfastness and patience have full play and do a thorough work, so that I may be perfectly and fully developed [with no defects], lacking in nothing. I will praise You with my whole heart; Your joy is my strength.

I determine to consider Him Who endured such opposition from sinful men, so that I will not grow weary and lose heart.

Father, Your grace is sufficient, and I will not grow weary in doing good, for at the proper time I will reap a harvest if I do not give up. I am strong in You, Lord, and in Your mighty power.

In the name of Jesus I pray, amen.[1]

Scripture References

Psalm 119:28 NIV	Psalm 27:1 AMP
Matthew 11:28-30 NIV	Psalm 3:3,4 AMP
1 Chronicles 16:11 NIV	James 1:2-4 AMP
Psalm 46:1 NIV	Psalm 9:1
Psalm 59:9,17 NIV	Nehemiah 8:10
Isaiah 40:29-31 NIV	Hebrews 12:3 NIV
Psalm 27:14 NIV	2 Corinthians 12:9
Exodus 15:2,13 NIV	Galatians 6:9 NIV
Isaiah 50:4 NIV	Ephesians 6:10 NIV

---

[1] For additional strength and guidance I suggest reading and meditating on the following passages: Psalm 6, Psalm 18, Psalm 27, Psalm 28, Psalm 38, Psalm 71.

40

Dealing With a Child With ADD/ADHD

Introduction

*I*n these last days Satan is working harder than ever to destroy our children. One of the areas of his attack is what psychologists and educators call Attention Deficit Disorder/Attention Deficit Hyperactivity Disorder. These disorders are tools of the enemy to disrupt households—causing confusion, frustration, division and every evil work. Their effects are far reaching.

Children and adults with ADD/ADHD are thought of as bullies, unruly, destructive, overbearing, impulsive, defiant— and the list goes on. It has been estimated that about two to five percent of school-aged children are now diagnosed with the disorder, and many adults who have it have never been diagnosed. Many who might be helped if properly diagnosed are in mental institutions, jails and prisons.[1]

---

[1] For additional information on ADD/ADHD including instructional practices for use in dealing with this disorder, see "101 Ways To Help Children With ADD Learn—Tips from Successful Teachers," published by Division of Innovation and Development, Office of Special Education Programs, Office of Special Education and Rehabilitative Services, U.S. Department of Education.

Although working with children diagnosed with ADD/ADHD can sometimes be frustrating and discouraging, as believers we know that God's Word, prayer, understanding caretakers, Christian counseling, medication and their peers can all help them become overcomers.

In our ministry to these special children, we must remember that, according to 2 Corinthians 10:4, **...the weapons of our warfare are not carnal, but mighty through God to the pulling down of strong holds.** Psalm 107:20 AMP says of the Lord's intervention on behalf of those in need, **He sends forth His word and heals them and rescues them from the pit and destruction.** Prayer, according to the Word of God, will avail much. (James 5:16.)

Declare and decree victory for the child as you teach and direct him/her through the following prayers.

The first two were written by a grandmother, one of our associates at Word Ministries, whose grandson has been diagnosed with ADD/ADHD. They pray together each morning before he leaves for school.

The third prayer and the following series of daily prayers were based on conversations and prayer times that I have had with this young man. He and I have cried and laughed together in my offices where we talk privately and confidentially.

At times, he asks to sit in a class where I am teaching, and later we discuss the subject matter. For instance, we may talk about abandonment issues and how Jesus felt when He was on the cross. He is not shy about asking for prayer when he is having a problem.

If you use any of these prayers, I encourage you when necessary to explain in simple language the meaning of the terms found in them. Remember, the child's imagination is creating pictures with the words he or she speaks and hears.

As the child prays, listen carefully, allowing him/her to express his/her feelings, fears, thoughts and ideas. Ask the Holy Spirit for discernment—it can be difficult to separate seriousness from horseplay. If you give the child time, he/she will let you know the difference.

Prayers To Be Prayed by the Child

I.

Coming Against ADD/ADHD

Father, in the name of Jesus, I come against ADD/ADHD and say that I have the mind of Christ (the Messiah) and hold the thoughts (feelings and purposes) of His heart; I am able to concentrate and stay focused on each task.

I am a disciple (taught by You, Lord, and obedient to Your will), and great is my peace and undisturbed composure. I do not have a spirit of fear, but [You have given me a spirit] of power and of love and of a calm, well-balanced mind and discipline and self-control.

In the name of Jesus, I come against my defiant behavior and tantrums and hyperactivity and speak peace and love to the situations in which I find myself. I cast down imaginations and every high thing that would exalt itself against the knowledge of You, Lord, and bring into captivity every thought to the obedience of Christ.

Father, I ask for Your wisdom to reside in me each day as I learn new techniques for handling stressful incidents.

Father, Your Word says not to worry about anything but to pray and ask You for everything I need and to give thanks when I pray, and Your peace will keep my heart and mind in Christ Jesus. The peace You give me is so great that I cannot understand it.

Thank You for keeping my mind quiet and at peace. I declare that I am an overcomer; I am in control.

In the name of Jesus, amen.

Scripture References

1 Corinthians 2:16 AMP   *Philippians 4:6,7* ICB

Isaiah 54:13 AMP   Isaiah 26:3

2 Timothy 1:7 AMP   Revelation 12:11

2 Corinthians 10:5

II.

Making New Friends

Father, I am asking You to supply me with good friends I can relate to, spend time with and enjoy as You intended. I desire to develop relationships that will be lasting and helpful to both me and my friends.

Father, I will keep sound-minded, self-restrained and alert—above all things I purpose to have intense and unfailing love for others, for I know love covers a multitude of sins [forgives and disregards the offenses of others].

I ask You to help me manage my behavior and attitude so others will want to be around me. I purpose to bridle my tongue and speak words of kindness. I will not insist on having my own way, and I will not act unbecomingly. When someone is unkind and falsely accuses me, help me to maintain a cool spirit and be slow to anger. I commit to plant seeds of love, and I thank You for preparing hearts ahead of time to receive me as a friend and as a blessing to their lives.

Father, thank You for causing me to find favor, compassion and loving-kindness with others.

Thank You, Lord, for my new friends.

In Jesus' name, amen.

Scripture References

1 Peter 4:7,8 AMP	James 1:19 AMP
Proverbs 21:23	1 Corinthians 3:6
1 Corinthians 13:4,5	Daniel 1:9 AMP
Proverbs 18:24 AMP	

III.

Having a Bad Day

Father, this was not a good day. My scores were low. It was a hard day for me at school and at home. I feel that I messed up a lot. Because I know that You love me unconditionally and You are not holding anything against me, I come to talk with You.

Father, You expect me to be accountable to You, my teachers and my parents for my behavior.[2] I ask Your

---

[2] NOTE TO PARENT: Effective reprimands should be brief and directed at the child's behavior, not at the character of the child. Direct him/her in assuming responsibility for his/her actions, acknowledging and asking forgiveness when appropriate.

forgiveness for acting mean and disrespectful to _____.
I acknowledge my misbehavior, and I ask You to forgive me
for _____.

Thank You, Lord, for helping me as I learn good
social skills and how to do unto others as I want them to
do unto me.

Father, I release my disappointment to You and believe
that tomorrow will be a great day! I look forward to the
new day with its new beginnings.

In the name of Jesus. Amen.

Scripture References

Romans 8:33-39 NIV	Matthew 15:4 NIV
2 Corinthians 5:18 TLB	1 John 1:9 TLB
Matthew 12:36 NIV	Luke 6:31 NIV
Romans 13:1-5 NIV	Proverbs 4:18

IV.
Living Each Day

MONDAY:

Father, in the name of Jesus, I thank You for giving
me life. You picked me out for Your very own even before

the foundation of the world—before I was ever born. You saw me while I was being formed in my mother's womb, and You know all about ADD/ADHD.

Lord, You see the weird things I do, and You know all my weird thoughts even before I think them. Thank You for loving me and helping me replace bad thoughts with good thoughts.

Help my parents, teachers—and, especially, the bus driver—to help me do right things. Help me to be kind to others.

In the name of Jesus, amen.

Scripture References

Ephesians 1:4 AMP   *Psalm 139:2* TLB

Psalm 139:13-16 TLB   *Ephesians 4:32* TLB

TUESDAY:

Father, Psalm 91 says that You have assigned angels to me—giving them [especial] charge over me to accompany and defend and preserve me in all my ways.

Lord, I need Your help. Sometimes my weird thoughts scare me, and I don't like the way I behave. I become so frightened and confused that I have to do something: run, make noises—even scream or try to hurt someone. These actions separate me from playmates; and when they don't want to be my friends, I am hurt and disappointed and angry.

I am asking You, Father, to help me form new behavior patterns and successfully overcome the disobedience and defiance that cause my parents and teachers anguish. I don't like to see them all upset, even though I laugh about it sometimes.

Thank You for helping me overcome obsessive, compulsive actions that create confusion for me and others around me. Even when others don't want me around, You will never abandon me. You will always be with me to help me and give me support.

In the name of Jesus, amen.

Scripture References

Psalm 91:11 AMP   Psalm 27:10 TLB

Romans 7:21-25 TLB   Hebrews 13:5 AMP

WEDNESDAY:

Father, thank You for my parents, grandparents, wise counselors and teachers who understand me and are helping me learn good behavior patterns. Help me to listen and develop good relationships with others—especially other children.

Thank You for giving me the ability to learn how to express my anger appropriately; I rejoice every time I have a victory. Your Son, Jesus, said that He has given me power to overcome all the obstacles that ADD/ADHD causes in my life.

In His name I pray, amen.

Scripture References

Ephesians 4:26 TLB   Luke 10:19 NIV

THURSDAY:

Father, I believe in my heart that Your Son, Jesus, is my Lord and Master and that He has come to live in my heart. Thank You for giving me the mind of Christ (the Messiah), His thoughts (feelings and purposes).

Lord, You are with me when my thoughts get jumbled up, and You have sent the Holy Spirit to help me concentrate and stay focused on each task at home and at school. I am a disciple [taught by You, Lord, and obedient to Your will], and great is my peace and undisturbed composure. Thank You for giving me Your helmet of salvation to protect my thought life.

In the name of Jesus, amen.

Scripture References

Romans 10:9,10 NIV   Isaiah 54:13 AMP

1 Corinthians 2:16 AMP   1 Thessalonians 5:8 NIV

John 16:13 NIV

FRIDAY:

Father, You have not given me a spirit of fear, but You have given me a spirit of power and of love and a calm, well-balanced mind and discipline and self-control. Thank You that as I grow in the grace and knowledge of Jesus Christ, You are creating in me a willing heart to be obedient.

Forgive me for throwing tantrums, and help me recognize and control the destructive ideas that cause them. The Holy Spirit is my Helper. Thank You for giving me the ability to channel hyperactivity in constructive, productive ways.

I choose to speak peace and love into the situations that confront me and make me feel uncomfortable and out of control.

In the name of Jesus, amen.

Scripture References

2 Timothy 1:7 AMP   Philippians 2:13

2 Peter 3:18   John 14:16 AMP

Exodus 35:5

SATURDAY:

Father, sometimes awful thoughts come to me, and I command the voices that tell me bad things to be quiet and leave me in the name of Jesus.

Lord, in Your Word You said that I can make choices. I choose to cast down imaginations that cause me to feel afraid and angry; these thoughts are not Your thoughts. You love me, and I will think on good things.

Father, I ask for Your wisdom to reside in me each day as I learn new techniques for handling stressful incidents.

In the name of Jesus, amen.

Scripture References

Deuteronomy 30:19,20 TLB   Isaiah 55:8 TLB

2 Corinthians 10:5   Philippians 4:8 TLB

SUNDAY:

Father, there are so many everyday things that worry and torment me. I feel so different from other people.

Lord, Your Word says not to worry about anything but to pray and ask You for everything I need and to give thanks when I pray, and Your peace will keep my heart and mind in Christ Jesus. The peace You give me is so great that I cannot understand it.

Thank You for keeping my mind quiet and at peace. I declare that I am an overcomer, and by submitting to Your control, I am learning self-control.

Father, I thank You for teaching me how to be a good friend to those You are sending to be my friends.

In the name of Jesus, amen.

Scripture References

Philippians 4:6,7 ICB	*Revelation 12:11*
Isaiah 26:3 AMP	*Galatians 5:23 AMP*

Prayer To Be Prayed by the Caregiver

Introduction

Caregivers of ADD/ADHD children often find themselves in situations that far exceed their parenting skills. Much prayer and faith are required to see the ADD/ADHD child as God sees him/her. The emotional turmoil and disruption to the household often become overwhelming, and caregivers sometimes discover that the challenges far exceed their natural ability.

Responsible adults involved in the life of an ADD/ADHD child need godly wisdom, spiritual discernment and mental and emotional alertness to overcome weariness, bewilderment and anxiety. Often, they second-guess themselves, processing confusing emotions and scenes of great conflict. Words spoken to the child and over him/her can comfort, giving him/her hope—or they can reinforce his/her belief that he/she is bad and that something terrible is wrong with him/her. Words can heal or words can wound.

The prayers of the ADD/ADHD child must be reinforced by those who love him/her. Often, our image of another individual—even our children—can only be changed as we pray according to God's will and purpose for him/her. The following personal prayer for the caregiver is a composite of things the Holy Spirit has directed me to pray for my friend and associate and her husband who are raising their ADD/ADHD grandson. I have observed in them the heartache, the delight, the exasperation—the full gamut of emotions involved in this challenging experience. But through it all, God is faithful!

Prayer

Father, in the name of Jesus, I thank You for this very special child. You see my confusion, anxiety; frustration and bewilderment as I attempt to rear him/her [tenderly] in the training and discipline and the counsel and admonition of the Lord. Forgive me for times when I knowingly or unknowingly irritate and provoke him/her to anger [exasperate him/her to resentment].

You see my intense pain when I observe the rejection this child suffers by adults who speak harsh words against him/her and our family. Children refuse to play with him/her, and it hurts even though I understand. I know that those who have never walked in our shoes cannot fully understand us.

But, Lord, where others are unmerciful and unkind, You are merciful and kind. Surely, goodness and mercy shall follow us all the days of our lives, and we shall dwell in Your house forever. Hide us in the secret place of Your presence and keep us secretly in Your pavilion from the strife of tongues.

Lord, perfect the fruit of my lips, that I may offer to You effective praise and thanksgiving for this child, who is a blessing from You. His/her intellect astounds me, and his/her wit is a delight. I ask You for divine intervention and guidance as I train him/her up in the way that he/she should go. I thank You for Your awesome handiwork and the techniques that You have given him/her to survive to overcome emotional turmoil—and the ability to function in this world around us. Truly, this child is fearfully and wonderfully made. I plead the blood of Jesus over him/her to protect him/her in every situation.

You have a divine purpose for this child. You have foreordained steps that he/she is to walk in, works that he/she is to do. Help me to look at his/her strengths and weaknesses realistically, that I may know how to help him/her develop and demonstrate self-control techniques. Forgive me for times when I lose patience and berate him/her for his/her behavior. Sometimes I lose sight of who he/she really is. Anoint my eyes to see him/her as You see him/her.

Father, help me to speak works of grace; anoint my lips to speak excellent and princely things over him/her, about him/her and to him/her. May the opening of my lips be for right things. Help me to give him/her healthy doses of unconditional love, administer to him/her appropriate discipline for misbehavior and reward him/her for his/her good behavior. Anoint my lips with coals of fire from Your altar, that I may speak words that comfort, encourage, strengthen and honor him/her. Keep watch at the door of my lips, and forgive me when my patience has come to an end.

Father, You are my Comforter, Counselor, Helper, Intercessor, Advocate, Strengthener and Standby. Whatever comes my way, help me to consider it wholly joyful, allowing endurance and steadfastness and patience to have full play and do a thorough work, so that I may be perfectly and fully developed [with no defects], lacking in nothing. When I am deficient in wisdom, I will ask of You, and You will give wisdom to me liberally and ungrudgingly, without reproaching or finding fault in me.

I pray that I may be invigorated and strengthened with all power according to the might of Your glory, [to exercise] every kind of endurance and patience (perseverance and forbearance) with joy.

Father, You have seen the tears in the night season, and I know that I shall experience the joy that comes in the morning times. You are my Exceeding Joy! You are my Wisdom, Righteousness, Sanctification and Redemption. Thank You for being a constant companion.

Lord, I see my child, _____, growing and becoming strong in spirit, increasing in wisdom (in broad and full understanding) and in stature and years and in favor with You and with man.

In the name of Jesus I pray. Amen.

Scripture References

Ephesians 6:4 AMP	Isaiah 6:6,7
Psalm 117:2	Psalm 141:3 AMP
Psalm 23:6	John 14:16 AMP
Psalm 31:20 AMP	James 1:2,4,5 AMP
Hebrews 13:15	Colossians 1:11 AMP
Psalm 127:3 AMP	Psalm 22:2
Proverbs 22:6	Psalm 30:5
Psalm 139:14	Psalm 43:4
Ephesians 2:10	1 Corinthians 1:30
Proverbs 8:6 AMP	Luke 1:80; 2:52 AMP

Daily Affirmations for Use by the Caregiver

Introduction

Often it is very difficult for ADD/ADHD children to learn, to develop new learning techniques in their lives and to change their negative behavior patterns. When working with them, it is so important that we love them with the God-kind of love and praise them for their accomplishments.

Following are examples of the kinds of positive daily affirmations that can be said to the ADD/ADHD child to help him/her develop a good self-image and to become all that God intends for him/her in this life.

Affirmations

• Great job • Well done • I'm very proud of you • Good for you • Neat • Outstanding • That was a smart decision • You are smart • God loves you • I love you • I knew you could do it • I believe in you • I know you are trying • Super-duper • You are a good boy/girl • Way to go • What an imagination • You are growing up • Good memory • Amazing • Nice work • What a wise choice • You are a blessing to me • You are special to me • You are valuable • You are a gem, a precious jewel • You are more precious than gold • You are incredible • You are important • Outstanding performance • You are a winner • Remarkable • Nothing can stop you • Now you've got it • Excellent • You are catching on • Great • Wonderful • Good • Terrific • Beautiful • Now you are cooking • You are fantastic • Beautiful work • Outstanding • You are spectacular • You are a real trooper • You are unique • Great discovery • You try so hard • Good try • Good effort • Magnificent • You've got it • Super work • Phenomenal • Marvelous • Dynamite • You mean so much to me • You make me laugh • You brighten my day • Hurray for you • You are beautiful • You are handsome • You are a good friend • You are a loving son/daughter [grandson/grand-daughter] • You light up my life • You belong • You are an important part of our family • We are family • You mean the world to me • That's right • You are correct • You are a success • Hurray • You are growing in wisdom every day • You are a beautiful creation • You are loved • I love you • Wow! • You are a success • You are an overcomer • You are a child of my love • You are victorious • You are a ray of sunshine • You are patient • You have a good attitude • You are a doer • You know how to get the job done • You are a chosen one • You give good hugs • Thank you for being a part of my life •

You are deserving of praise!

Scripture Passages for Meditation

A GOOD REPORT:	*Proverbs 15:30; Philippians 4:8*
A SOFT ANSWER:	*Proverbs 15:1*
PERFECT LOVE:	*1 John 4:18*

PART II

Group Prayers

An Intercessory
Prayer Group

Introduction

*I*ntercessory prayer groups are made up of real people with real problems. They are individuals who are willing to lay aside their personal needs and pray for others.

Over the years many women of God have come to Word Ministries, Inc., sincerely desiring to learn more about intercessory prayer. God has preserved a remnant that has remained loyal and faithful. We appreciate the diversity of personalities that make up our prayer group, making room for one another's distinctive traits and gifts. Each individual faces challenges (trials, tribulations and temptations) that differ one from the other. Understanding each other's uniqueness enables us to love one another and to pray more effectively.

In a group such as ours, it is tempting sometimes to please others rather than God. [We] **watch and pray, that [we] enter not into temptation...** (Matt. 26:41) and miss God's purpose and plan. We do not always hear the same thing, and we have learned the importance of good communication and are seeking to practice **...speaking the truth in love...** (Eph. 4:15).

This has become a safe place for us where God is able to deal with us as individuals in a Christian community.

We are experiencing love, encouragement, healing and growth on a level that was not possible when we were emotionally isolated, trying to do everything by ourselves. We allow each other to be a human being with needs and imperfections, while at the same time acknowledging that the One God and Father lives in us all. (Eph. 4:6 AMP.)

As we grow in intimacy, brotherly affection, we are able to comfort those for whom we pray with the comfort that we receive from the Lord. (2 Cor. 1:3,4.) Today, prayer requests are received and responded to by a group that is increasingly more sensitive to the needs of the people and to the prompting of the Holy Spirit. We are not merely concerned with our own interests, but also with the interests of others. (Phil. 2:4 NIV.)

41

Individual Growth

*F*ather, in the name of Jesus, we in our prayer group desire that our prayers avail much. We are individuals who are [mutually dependent on one another], having gifts (faculties, talents, qualities) that differ according to the grace given us. We, who with unveiled faces all reflect Your glory, are being transformed into Your likeness with ever-increasing glory, which comes from You, Who are the Spirit.

Father, we realize that You know what we have need of before we ask and that we are not all growing in the same manner or on the same time schedule, but we are growing in the grace and knowledge of our Lord and Savior, Jesus Christ.

We give each other space to grow, for we are becoming a patient people, bearing with one another and making allowances because we love one another. We acknowledge that we do not have dominion [over] each other, and we refuse to lord it over one another's faith, but we are fellow laborers [to promote] one another's joy, because it is by faith that we stand firm.

In Jesus' name, amen.

Scripture References

James 5:16   2 Peter 3:18

Romans 12:5,6 AMP   2 Corinthians 1:24 AMP

2 Corinthians 3:18 NIV   Ephesians 4:20

Matthew 6:32

42

A Group Member Experiencing Grief or Loss

*F*ather, in the name of Jesus, we approach Your throne of grace, bringing _____ before You. We recognize that grieving is a human emotional process, and we give him/her the space that he/she needs to enter into the rest that You have for him/her.

Lord, Jesus bore _____'s griefs (sicknesses, weaknesses and distresses) and carried his/her sorrows and pains; we know that Your Spirit is upon Jesus to bind up and heal _____'s broken heart. May he/she be gentle with himself/herself, knowing that he/she is not alone in his/her grief. You are with him/her, and You will never leave him/her without support.

Give us, _____'s friends and prayer partners, discernment, sympathy and understanding so that we may bear (endure, carry) his/her burden of loss. We trust You to guide him/her, and we respect his/her decisions, awaiting the manifestation of Your healing.

Father, we desire to be doers of Your Word, and not hearers only. Therefore, we make a commitment to rejoice with those who rejoice [sharing others' joy], and to weep with those who weep [sharing others' grief]. We pray that our love will give _____ great joy and comfort and encouragement, because he/she has cheered and refreshed the hearts of Your people.

Thank You, Father, for sending the Holy Spirit to comfort, counsel, help, intercede for, defend, strengthen and stand by _____ in this time of grief and sorrow.

In Jesus' name, amen.

Scripture References

Isaiah 53:4 AMP	James 1:22
Isaiah 61:1 AMP	Romans 12:15 AMP
Hebrews 13:5 AMP	Philemon 7 AMP
Galatians 6:2 AMP	John 14:26 AMP

43

Loving and Caring for Self

*F*ather, I realize that before I can love others as You have instructed, I must love myself. Help me to speak truly, deal truly and live truly in harmony with You, myself and others in my prayer group.

I am Your workmanship, created in Christ Jesus. I am fearfully and wonderfully made. Help me to remember that others do not always know what is best for me. I trust in You with all my heart and lean not on my own understanding; in all my ways I acknowledge You, and You will make my paths straight.

I look to You to cause my thoughts to be agreeable to Your will, that I may make healthy choices. Give me the courage to say no when it is in my best interest according to Your purpose and plan for my life.

I take responsibility for myself and allow others in our prayer group to take responsibility for themselves, in the name of Jesus. This frees me so that I am not [merely] concerned with my own interests, but also with the interests of others.

I desire to do unto others as I would have them do unto me. I am walking uprightly before You; therefore, I consider, direct and establish my way [with the confidence of integrity].

You are my confidence, and You will keep my foot from being snared. Your love is shed abroad in my heart, and I will love my neighbor as myself.

In Jesus' name, amen.

Scripture References

Romans 13:9	Philippians 2:4 AMP
Ephesians 4:15 AMP	Matthew 7:12
Ephesians 2:10	Proverbs 21:29 AMP
Psalm 139:14	Proverbs 3:26
Proverbs 3:5,6 NIV	Romans 5:5
Proverbs 16:3 AMP	Matthew 22:39

44

Perseverance in Prayer

*F*ather, the course that You have set before me is clear. You have called me into this prayer group to respond to the many prayer requests we receive from those who need agreement or who don't know how to pray for themselves.

Lord, You are the Vinedresser; Jesus is the Vine; and I am the branch. I remain in Him and He remains in me, and my prayers bear much fruit; apart from Him, I can do nothing.

Father, at times I am tempted to grow weary and overburdened with the pain and heartache of others. Help me to remember that Jesus said, **"Come to me, all you who are weary and burdened, and I will give you rest"** (Matt. 11:28 NIV). I take His yoke upon me and learn from Him, for He is gentle and humble in heart, and I will find rest for my soul. His yoke is easy, and His burden is light.

Lord, Jesus said that I ought always to pray and not to turn coward (faint, lose heart and give up). I am earnest and unwearied and steadfast in my prayer [life], being [both] alert and intent [in my praying with thanksgiving].

Therefore, since I am surrounded by such a great cloud of witnesses, I throw off everything that hinders and the sin that so easily entangles, and I run with perseverance the race marked out for me. I fix my eyes on Jesus, the author and perfecter of my faith, Who for the joy set before Him endured the cross, scorning its shame, and sat down at the right hand of Your throne. I consider Him Who endured such opposition from sinful men, so that I will not grow weary and lose heart during times of intercession.

In His name I pray. Amen.

Scripture References

John 15:1-7 AMP

Colossians 4:2 AMP

Matthew 11:29,30 NIV

Hebrews 12:1-3 NIV

Luke 18:1 AMP

45

Pleasing God Rather Than Men

*F*ather, I desire to please You rather than men. Forgive me for loving the approval and the praise and the glory that come from men [instead of and] more than the glory that comes from You. [I value my credit with You more than credit with men.]

In Jesus' name I declare that I am free from the fear of man, which brings a snare. I lean on, trust in and put my confidence in You. I am safe and set on high.

I take comfort and am encouraged and confidently and boldly say, "The Lord is my Helper; I will not be seized with alarm [I will not fear or dread or be terrified]. What can man do to me?"

Father, just as You sent Jesus into the world, You have sent me. You are ever with me, for I always seek to do what pleases You.

In Jesus' name, amen.

Scripture References

John 12:43 AMP

Proverbs 29:25 AMP

Hebrews 13:6 AMP

John 17:18 AMP

John 8:29 AMP

46

Communication With Group Members

*F*ather, to as many as received Jesus, You gave the power to become Your sons and daughters. I am learning to be straightforward in my communication with my brothers and sisters in Christ, my co-laborers in the Lord. I have the power to be direct, honestly expressing my feelings and desires because Jesus has been made unto me wisdom. Wisdom from above is straightforward, impartial (unbiased, objective) and unfeigned (free from doubts, wavering and insincerity).

I am Your creation, Father, and You created me to be active in sharing my faith, so that I will have a full understanding of every good thing we have in Christ. It is my prayer in Jesus' name that my conversation will always be full of grace, seasoned with salt, so that I may know how to answer everyone. I am content with my own reality (satisfied to the point where I am not disturbed or disquieted) in whatever state I am, so those around me can feel safe in my presence. I will speak truly, deal truly and live truly, expressing the truth in love.

As Your children and co-laborers, we walk in the ever-developing maturity that enables us to be in perfect harmony and full agreement in what we say, perfectly united in our common understanding and in our opinions and judgments. And if on some point we think differently, You will make it clear to us. We live up to what we have already attained in our individual lives and in our group. We will let our yes be simply yes, and our no be simply no.

In Jesus' name, amen.

Scripture References

John 1:12	Philippians 4:11 AMP
1 Corinthians 1:30	Ephesians 4:15 AMP
James 3:17 AMP	1 Corinthians 1:10 AMP
Philemon 6 NIV	Philippians 3:15-17 NIV
Colossians 4:6 NIV	Matthew 5:37 AMP

Ministries

47

Prayers for Ministry Partners

Introduction

*O*ur ministry, Word Ministries, Inc., is a prayer ministry dedicated to uniting people of the Christian faith for the purpose of praying God's will into the earth for all nations. The effectual fervent prayer of the righteous has great power and wonderful results when prayed according to God's will. (James 5:16.)

In our ministry we correspond with and pray for people around the world, conduct prayer schools and continue to write scriptural prayers for many situations. During these last days, networks of intercessors are reaching out in a cooperative effort to bring God to the nations.

The Lord has worked out a plan for financing His work in the earth. As our part of that plan, we send letters of acknowledgment to everyone who gives into this ministry. The following are prayers written especially for our contributors. They may be prayed for the partners of any ministry.

I.

Father, we thank You for _____ and for his/her service and dedication to serve You. We thank You that he/she brings forth the fruit of the Spirit: love, joy, peace, longsuffering, gentleness, goodness, faith, meekness and temperance.

_____ is Your creation of love and has been crucified with Christ: Nevertheless, he/she lives; yet not he/she, but Christ lives in him/her. And the life that _____ now lives in the flesh, he/she lives by the faith of the Son of God, Who loved him/her and gave Himself for him/her.

Father, we thank You that _____ is good ground, that he/she hears Your Word and understands it and that the Word bears fruit in his/her life. He/she is like a tree planted by the rivers of water, bringing forth fruit in its season. His/her leaf shall not wither, and whatever he/she does, in the name of Jesus, shall prosper.

Thank You, Father, for filling _____ with the knowledge of Your will in all wisdom and spiritual understanding, that he/she may walk worthy of You, Lord, being fruitful in every good work and increasing in the knowledge of You. _____ is merciful, as his/her Father is merciful. Because he/she doesn't judge other people, he/she will not be judged. He/she does not

condemn, and he/she will not be condemned. _____
forgives others, and people forgive him/her. _____
gives, and men will give to him/her—yes, good measure,
pressed down, shaken together and running over will they
pour into his/her lap. For whatever measure he/she uses with
other people, they will use in their dealings with him/her.

In Jesus' name we pray, amen.

Scripture References

Galatians 5:22,23   Psalm 1:3

Galatians 2:20   Colossians 1:9

Mark 4:8   Luke 6:36-38 PHILLIPS

II.

Father, it is our prayer that good will come to
_____. He/she is generous and lends freely. He/she
conducts his/her affairs with justice.

Lord, Your Word says that surely _____ will
never be shaken. He/she is a righteous man/woman who
will be remembered forever. He/she will have no fear of
bad news; his/her heart is steadfast, trusting in You, Lord.

_____'s heart is secure, he/she will have no fear;
in the end he/she will look in triumph on his/her foes.

He/she has scattered abroad his/her gifts to the poor; his/her righteousness endures forever; his/her horn will be lifted high in honor.

We pray that Your plans will be fulfilled in _____'s life, and we thank You for Your mercies on his/her behalf.

In the name of Jesus, amen.

Scripture References

Psalm 112:5-9 *NIV*   Jeremiah 29:11 *NIV*

48

Office Staff

Introduction

*O*ur prayer coordinator wrote this prayer for our ministry. It may be used for the members of any ministry or outreach that depends upon the Holy Spirit to go before it and prepare the way for its labor with and for the Lord.

Prayer

Father, we begin this day rejoicing in You. We thank You for Your goodness, mercy and grace toward us as individuals and as a ministry. We confess and proclaim that this is the day that You have made, and we purpose to rejoice and be glad in it.

Father, we lift up the day with its activities, its relationships, its decisions and creativity. We offer it all up to You, acknowledging Jesus as Lord of all and asking You by Your Holy Spirit to use it for Your glory and honor. We pray for Your will to be done in us individually and as a ministry.

We plead the blood of Jesus over this property, all staff members, every telephone contact, every person who enters these doors and the entire ministry network, including all those for whom we pray. We thank You for delivering us from the authority of darkness and translating us into the Kingdom of Your dear Son. We are living and growing up in the Kingdom of light.

Father, You have given us choices. We choose life and blessings. You are our Strength, our Confidence and our Courage. We are courageous, boldly proclaiming that Your anointing—Your burden-removing, yoke-destroying power—is abiding in us individually and collectively. This anointing is working in, on and through us this day to accomplish Your will. May You be glorified in all that we do.

Thank You for Your love. We are imitators of You—walking in love, in truth, in light and in wisdom inside and outside these offices. We are well-balanced and enduring in all things.

We are asking for and expecting the former and latter rains to be poured out on this ministry to fulfill Your assignments. You have called us by Your grace for such a time as this. We rejoice in the outpouring of Your Spirit on this ministry.

In the name of Jesus, amen.

Scripture References

Psalm 33:1	1 John 2:27
Psalm 118:24	1 Corinthians 6:20
1 Corinthians 12:3	Ephesians 5:1,2 AMP
Matthew 6:10	James 5:7
Colossians 1:13	1 Peter 5:10
Deuteronomy 30:19	Esther 4:14
Isaiah 10:27	Acts 2:17

49

Overcoming Prejudice

Introduction

*T*he previous few days in Miami had been exceptionally cool. Jan, my traveling companion, and I did not consider it coat weather, but the Floridians shivered, all bundled up in their winter wear.

The prayer seminar had gone well, and it was now our last service before leaving for home. The preparation for the Sunday morning worship service had been difficult, and I found myself at the mercy of the Holy Spirit. (Not a bad place to be!)

During the preliminaries and the praise and worship service, I was crying out inwardly, just for a starting Scripture that I could read.

The sanctuary was packed as I stood before the congregation of beautiful skin tones—from almost white to light chocolate to black velvet. Their faces looked back at me. I smiled and began to read a psalm, making comments as I felt prompted by the Holy Spirit.

Where is the flow of the Spirit? I wondered. *God, what is it You want to do in this church today?*

The tension within me grew, and I felt helpless.

At last, I knew. (Sometimes it is good that we do not know what we will say beforehand. We might mess it all up, working to be politically correct, writing and rewriting to make sure that we cross every "t" and dot every "i" with the correct flourish.)

The love of God began to rise within me. I spoke from my heart of hearts:

"You cannot really know me unless I choose to share myself—my thoughts, my ideas and my feelings. Obviously, I am a Southern white woman. I grew up in cotton mill towns in North Georgia. There I attended the all-white Pentecostal churches where my dad served as pastor. I attended all-white schools and lived in all-white neighborhoods. The only black people I knew were Smut and Clarabell, tenants on my uncle's farm.

"I don't know if I have any racial prejudice—it has never been tested. I know that at one time I was filled with intellectual prejudice, because God exposed it in a very dramatic way. If I have any racial prejudice, I want the Holy Spirit to uncover it and deliver me. All I know is that I love you, and we are one—one blood. In Christ Jesus there is neither Jew nor Greek, male nor female, black nor white. There is that one new man created in Him."

The barriers came tumbling down. My newly found friends, brothers and sisters in the Lord, no longer hugged from a distance. Many smothered me in bear hugs after the benediction. The unity of the Spirit had prevailed. (Eph. 4:3.)

Jesus is our peace, and I believe that the Scriptures written by the Apostle Paul in Galatians and Ephesians apply today.

Ethnic groups are assuming responsibility for the sins of the forefathers and asking forgiveness for past wrongs done to one another. We are accountable to God and each other as members of one household, and by the blood of the Lamb and through good communication we are overcoming the dividing schemes of the devil. God is bringing His people together. Red and yellow, black and white—we are coming together—and we are precious in His sight.

We are no longer outsiders or aliens, but fellow citizens with every other Christian—we belong now to the household of God. (Eph. 2:19 PHILLIPS.)

Prayer

Father, in the name of Jesus, we come before You, asking Your forgiveness for being intolerant of one another because of the colors of our skin. Forgive us for tolerating prejudice in the household of faith. Set us free from the influence of public opinion, that we may live out our glorious, Christ-originated faith.

Forgive us for segregating ourselves by color, by a measure of wealth or intellect. We are all Your children, the sheep of Your pasture. You made us, and not we ourselves.

We are one blood, redeemed by the blood of the Lamb, Who was slain before the foundation of the world. We are baptized "into" Christ and have put on the family likeness of Christ.

We call for an end to division and segregation in Christ's family—may there be no division into Jew and non-Jew, slave and free, male and female. Among us we are all equal. That is, we are all in a common relationship with Jesus Christ.

Thank You, Father, for bringing us together in Christ through His death on the cross. The cross got us to embrace, and that was the end of the hostility.

Lord, Jesus came and preached peace to us outsiders and peace to us insiders. He treated us as equals, and so made us equals. Through Him we share the same Spirit and have equal access to You, Father.

The Kingdom of faith is now our home country, and we are no longer strangers or outsiders. We *belong* here.

Lord, You are building a home. You are using us all—irrespective of how we got here—in what You are building. You are fitting us in with Christ Jesus as the Cornerstone Who holds all the parts together. We see it taking shape day after day—a holy temple built by You, Father, all of us built into it, a temple in which You are quite at home.

Father, You have called us all to travel on the same road and in the same direction, so we will stay together, both outwardly and inwardly. We have one Master, one faith, one baptism, one God and Father of all—Who rules over all, works through all and is present in all. Everything we are and think and do is permeated with oneness.

Father, we imitate You. We walk in love, [esteeming and delighting in one another]. We walk as children of the light [leading the lives of those native-born to the light]. We look carefully how we walk! We live purposefully and worthily and accurately, making the very most of the time [buying up each opportunity], because the days are evil.

We speak out to one another in psalms and hymns and spiritual songs, offering praise with voice [and instruments] and making melody with all our hearts to You, Lord, at all times and for everything giving thanks in the name of our Lord Jesus Christ to You, Father. By love we serve one another.

Thank You, Father, that prejudice is being rooted out of the Body of Christ, in the name of Jesus. Amen.

Scripture References

James 2:1 MESSAGE

Psalm 100:3

1 Peter 1:18 NIV

Galatians 3:27 PHILLIPS

Galatians 3:28 MESSAGE

Ephesians 2:13-22 MESSAGE

Ephesians 4:3-6 MESSAGE

Ephesians 5:1,2,8 AMP

Ephesians 5:15,16,19,20 AMP

Galatians 5:13 AMP

50

A Ministry in Need of Finances

Introduction

*T*his prayer was written in response to an appeal for help from a ministry in a financial crunch. This ministry reaches out to people addicted to drugs, alcohol and other substances, and then out beyond the youths and adults to their families. After we had prayed the following prayer, it was given to our editor and prayer request correspondent. It can be used to pray for the needs of any ministry.

Prayer

Father, in the name of Jesus, we believe that all of the needs of _____ are met, according to Philippians 4:19. We believe that—because this ministry has given tithes and offerings to further Your cause to help youth, adults and families come to the knowledge of the truth—[gifts] will be given to them; good measure, pressed down, shaken together and running over will they be poured into their bosom. For with the measure they deal out, it will be measured back to them.

Father, in the name of Jesus, we pray, confess and believe according to Your Word that those in Your Body who have sown [the seed of] spiritual good among the people will reap from the people's material benefits, for You have directed that those who publish the good news of the Gospel should live and get their maintenance by the Gospel.

We confess that Your ministers with _____ Ministry seek and are eager for the fruit that increases to the people's credit [the harvest of blessing that is accumulating to their account]. The people's gifts are the fragrant odor of an offering and sacrifice that You, Father, welcome and in which You delight. You will liberally supply (fill to the full) the people's every need according to Your riches in glory in Christ Jesus.

Father, we call forth partners who will respond to Your call to support this ministry prayerfully and financially.

Lord, we thank You for directing the leader, _____, who seeks Your ways, teaching him/her the fortitude of Your Word and the steadfastness of its truth. Your anointing, which destroys the yoke of bondage, abides within him/her permanently. Teach him/her to pray for the people and the government of our land. We thank

You for Your Word, which brings freedom to the hearers, and we thank You for preparing their hearts to receive the good news of the Gospel.

Lord, strengthen (complete, perfect) and make _____ what he/she ought to be, equipping him/her with everything good, that he/she may carry out Your will; [while You Yourself] work in him/her and accomplish that which is pleasing in Your sight, through Jesus Christ (the Messiah), to Whom be the glory forever and ever (to the ages of the ages).

In His name we pray, amen.

Scripture References

Luke 6:38 AMP	*Isaiah 10:27*
1 Corinthians 9:11,13 AMP	*1 Timothy 2:1-3 AMP*
Philippians 4:17-19 AMP	*John 8:32*
Matthew 9:38 AMP	*Hebrews 13:21 AMP*

51

Ministry in Nursing Homes

*F*ather, thank You for calling me to minister to Your children in nursing homes. I purpose to keep on going by Your power, for You first saved me and then called me to this holy work. I had nothing to do with it. It was Your idea, a gift prepared for me in Jesus long before I knew anything about it.

But I know it now. Since the appearance of our Savior, nothing could be plainer; death defeated, life vindicated in a steady blaze of light—all through the work of Jesus. I couldn't be more sure of my ground—the One I've trusted in can take care of what He's trusted me to do right to the end.

Thank You for Your Word—the entrance of Your Word brings light, and Your light is the life of men. The words that I speak are spirit and life, and I pray that the light of the Gospel will illumine the minds of those to whom I minister.

Father, Your anointing abides within me [permanently]—thank You for [an unction from] the Holy One.

You have touched my hands with Your anointing, and when I lay hands on the sick, they shall experience the healing that flows from Your throne and recover.

Thank You, Lord, for those who welcome me, reaching out for prayer, encouragement and hugs. I pray that the light in my eyes will bring joy to their hearts. Help me to exhort and teach them to continue in their desire to be useful, fulfilling Your call on their lives.

Father, You have a purpose for them—it is not Your will that they be set aside. You want them to continue bringing forth fruit in their old age. Help me to bring understanding to them.

Oh, Father, I pray for those who are in fetal positions, not speaking or opening their eyes. Arise, O Sun of righteousness, with healing in Your wings and minister to these souls who will soon meet You face-to-face. I yield my body to You to be used as an instrument of righteousness, bringing salvation, wholeness, healing, deliverance and comfort to the sick and the elderly.

Father, You execute justice for the fatherless and the widow, and You are a judge and protector (champion) of the widow. You protect, preserve and uphold the fatherless and widow, and You set them upright. I am claiming these promises for all those I minister to, believing You to watch over Your Word to perform it.

Lord, Your arm is not shortened that You cannot save, and nothing is too hard for You. I ask You for the wisdom and common sense I need to be a vessel of honor, sanctified and fitting for Your use and prepared for every good work.

I do not go in my own strength, but in the divine energy that You provide. It is my purpose to always be obedient to James 1:27 AMP—**External religious worship... that is pure and unblemished in the sight of God the Father is this: to visit and help and care for the orphans and widows in their affliction and need...**—and to reach out to the homeless and loveless in their plight.

Thank You, Lord, that I eat the good of the land because I am willing and obedient. I serve You with a glad heart and a joyous spirit. Whatever You call me to do, You equip me with all that I need to accomplish it.

In the name of Jesus, amen.

Scripture References

2 Timothy 1:8-10 MESSAGE   Deuteronomy 10:18 AMP

Psalm 119:130   Psalm 68:5 AMP

John 1:4   Psalm 146:9 AMP

John 6:63   Jeremiah 1:12 AMP

2 Corinthians 4:4 AMP   Isaiah 39:1

1 John 2:20,27 AMP   Genesis 18:14

Mark 16:18   James 1:15

Psalm 92:14   2 Timothy 2:21

Mark 4:2   Isaiah 1:19

Romans 6:13

52

A Christian Counselor

*F*ather, in the name of Jesus, I pray for _____ to exhort and counsel the emotionally wounded. I ask in faith that Your Spirit will rest upon him/her—the Spirit of wisdom and understanding, the Spirit of counsel and might. Give him/her insight and knowledge for understanding his/her counselees' responses to circumstances.

Thank You, Father, that _____ is a good listener to the confessions of his/her counselees. Help him/her to comprehend the unfolding of those past hurts that influence reactions to current situations.

Lord, _____ will not judge by what he/she sees with his/her eyes or decide by what he/she hears with his/her ears. He/she will judge the needy and give decisions with justice. Righteousness will be his/her belt, and faithfulness the sash around his/her waist. He/she will be clothed with fairness and with truth.

Thank You that _____ is a promoter of peace and is filled with joy. Grant Your counselor, out of the rich treasury of Your glory, to be strengthened and reinforced with mighty power in the inner man by the [Holy] Spirit [Himself indwelling his/her innermost being and personality].

You will not leave _____ without support as he/she gives his/her time and concern, helping to complete the forgiveness process. He/she will be confident about his/her convictions, knowing excellent things, and will have the knowledge to assist Your children in knowing the certainty of the words of truth.

In Jesus' name, amen.

Scripture References

Isaiah 11:2,3   Ephesians 3:16 *AMP*

Isaiah 11:4,5 *NIV*   Proverbs 22:20,21 *AMP*

Isaiah 11:5 *TLB*

Peoples and Nations

53

The People of Our Land

*F*ather, in the name of Jesus, we come before You to claim Your promise in 2 Chronicles 7:14 AMP: **If My people, who are called by My name shall humble themselves, pray, seek, crave, and require of necessity My face and turn from their wicked ways, then will I hear from heaven, forgive their sin, and heal their land.**

We are Your people, called by Your name. Thank You for hearing our prayers and moving by Your Spirit in our land. There are famines, earthquakes, floods, natural disasters and violence occurring. Men's hearts are failing them because of fear.

Lord, Your Son, Jesus, spoke of discerning the signs of the times. With the Holy Spirit as our Helper, we are watching and praying.

We desire to humble ourselves before You, asking that a spirit of humility be released in us. Thank You for quiet and meek spirits, for we know that the meek shall inherit the earth.

Search us, O God, and know our hearts; try us, and know our thoughts today. See if there be any wicked way in us, and lead us in the way everlasting.

Forgive us our sins of judging inappropriately, complaining about and criticizing our leaders. Cleanse us with hyssop, and we will be clean; wash us, and we will be whiter than snow. Touch our lips with coals from Your altar, that we may pray prayers that avail much for all men and women everywhere.

Lord, we desire to release rivers of living water for the healing of the nations.

In the name of Jesus, amen.

Scripture References

Luke 21:11,25,26	*Psalm 51:7 NIV*
Matthew 16:3	*Isaiah 6:6,7 NIV*
Matthew 26:41	*James 5:16*
James 4:10	*1 Timothy 2:1*
1 Peter 3:4	*John 7:38*
Matthew 5:5	*Revelation 22:1,2*
Psalm 139:23	

54

Members of the Armed Forces[1]

*F*ather, our troops have been sent into _____ as peace keepers. We petition You, Lord, according to Psalm 91, for the safety of our military personnel.

This is no afternoon athletic contest that our armed forces will walk away from and forget about in a couple of hours. This is for keeps, a life-or-death fight to the finish against the devil and all his angels. We look beyond human instruments of conflict and address the forces and authorities and rulers of darkness and powers in the spiritual world. As children of the Most High God we enforce the triumphant victory of our Lord, Jesus Christ.

Jesus stripped you, Satan, of your principalities and powers, making a show of you openly. Our Lord and Master defeated you. All power and authority both in heaven and earth belong to Him. Righteousness and truth shall prevail. Nations shall come to the light of the Gospel.

---

[1] A portion of this prayer was taken from a letter dated January 22, 1996, written by Kenneth Copeland of Kenneth Copeland Ministries in Fort Worth, Texas, and sent to his partners. Used by permission.

We petition heaven to turn our troops into a real peace-keeping force by pouring out the glory of God through our men and women in that part of the world. Use them as instruments of righteousness to defeat the plans of the devil.

Lord, we plead the power of the blood of Jesus, asking You to manifest Your power and glory. We entreat You on behalf of the citizens in these countries on both sides of this conflict. They have experienced pain and heartache; they are victims of the devil's strategies to steal, kill and destroy. We pray that they will come to know Jesus, Who came to give us life and life more abundantly.

We stand in the gap for the people of the war-torn, devil-overrun land. We expect an overflowing of Your goodness and glory in the lives of those for whom we are praying. May they call upon Your name and be saved.

You, Lord, make known Your salvation; Your righteousness You openly show in the sight of the nations.

Father, provide for and protect the families of our armed forces. Preserve marriages; cause the hearts of the parents to turn toward their children and the hearts of the children to turn toward the fathers and mothers. We plead the blood of Jesus over our troops and their families. Provide a support system to undergird, uplift and edify those who have been left to raise children by themselves.

Jesus has been made unto these parents wisdom, righteousness and sanctification. Through Your Holy Spirit, comfort the lonely and strengthen the weary.

Father, we are looking forward to that day when the whole earth shall be filled with the knowledge of the Lord as the waters cover the sea.

In Jesus' name, amen.

Scripture References

Ephesians 6:12 MESSAGE	Psalm 98:2 AMP
Colossians 2:15	Malachi 4:6
John 10:10	1 Corinthians 1:30
Ezekiel 22:30	Isaiah 11:9
Acts 2:21	

55

The Nation and People of Israel

*L*ord, You will not cast off nor spurn Your people; neither will You abandon Your heritage. You have regard for the covenant [You made with Abraham]. Father, remember Your covenant with Abraham, Isaac and Jacob.

Father, we pray for the peace of Jerusalem. May they prosper who love you [the Holy City]. May peace be within your walls and prosperity within your palaces! For our brethren and companions' sake, we will now say, "Peace be within you!" For the sake of the house of the Lord our God, we will seek, inquire for and require your good.

Father, we thank You for bringing the people of Israel into unity with each other and for bringing Your Church (both Jew and Gentile) into oneness—one new man. Thank You for the peace treaties with Israel's former enemies. May these treaties be used for good to make way for the good news of the Gospel as we prepare for the coming of our Messiah.

We intercede for those who have become callously indifferent (blinded, hardened and made insensible to the Gospel). We pray that they will not fall to their utter spiritual ruin. It was through their false step and transgression that salvation has come to the Gentiles. Now, we ask that the eyes of their understanding be enlightened, that they may know the Messiah, Who will make Himself known to all of Israel.

We ask You to strengthen the house of Judah and save the house of Joseph. Thank You, Father, for restoring them because You have compassion on them. They will be as though You had not rejected them, for You are the Lord their God, and You will answer them. We thank You for Your great mercy and love to them and to us, in the name of Yeshua, our Messiah.

Father, thank You for saving Israel and gathering them from the nations, that they may give thanks to Your holy name and glory in Your praise. Praise be to You, Lord, the God of Israel, from everlasting to everlasting. Let all the people say, "Amen!" Praise the Lord.

In Jesus' name, amen.

Scripture References

Psalm 94:14 AMP · Romans 11:7 AMP

Psalm 74:20 AMP · Romans 11:11 AMP

Leviticus 46:22 · Ephesians 1:18

Psalm 122:6-9 AMP · Zechariah 10:6,12 NIV

Ephesians 2:14 AMP · Psalm 106:47,48 NIV

Special Needs
of Others

56

Those Involved in Abortion

Introduction

*T*hrough our ministry, a dear child of God shared with us the following Scriptures, which continue to bring her through periods of grief and sorrow. God's grace and love have proven to be the balm necessary for healing the emotional pain incurred by an act that cannot be reversed. The memory of the decision will never be erased. Reminders are all around—at church, in the media and in everyday life.

The prayer as written has a two-fold application: (1) for a people—a nation—who has permitted the legalization of abortion on demand; (2) for both the man and woman involved in the decision-making process. During moments of intercession for women and men who are dealing with past mistakes, we have identified with them in their pain. God's Word is the medicine that heals and the salvation of souls.

Prayer[1]

Father, in the name of Jesus, forgive us as a nation for disregarding the sanctity of life. We recognize that each person is uniquely created by You, Lord—marvelously made! You know each one inside and out, You know every bone in the body. You know exactly how we are made, bit by bit, how we are sculpted from nothing into something. All the stages of a life are spread out before you, and the days are prepared before a child even lives one day. Since we now see clearly, we value the life You give.

Father, each of us is an open book to You; even from a distance, You know what we are thinking. We are never out of Your sight. When we look back, we realize that You were there. You were present when we put to death the being/beings to whom You gave life.

Lord, we repent of our sin and the sin of our nation. Be merciful unto us, O Lord. We ask Your forgiveness, and You are faithful and just to forgive us and cleanse us from all unrighteousness.

Unless Your law had been our delight, we would have perished in our affliction. We will never forget Your precepts, [how can we?] for it is by them You have quickened us (granted us life).

---

[1] This prayer can also be prayed in the singular "I" form by the individual person involved in abortion.

We are ready to halt and fall; our pain and sorrow are continually before us. For we do confess our guilt and iniquity; we are filled with sorrow for our sin.

So [instead of further rebuke, now] we desire rather to turn and be [graciously] forgiven and comforted and encouraged to keep us from being overwhelmed by excessive sorrow and despair.

We look to Jesus as our Savior and Consolation and welcome His peace and completeness to our souls. We cannot bring our child/children back again; we shall go to them; they will not return to us.

We are awaiting and looking for the [fulfillment, the realization of our] blessed hope, even the glorious appearing of our great God and Savior, Christ Jesus (the Messiah, the Anointed One).

In His name we pray, amen.

Scripture References

Psalm 139:14-16 MESSAGE	Psalm 38:17,18 AMP
Psalm 139:2-5 MESSAGE	2 Corinthians 2:7 AMP
1 John 1:9	2 Samuel 12:23 AMP
Psalm 119:92,93 AMP	Titus 2:13 AMP

57

An *AIDS Patient*

I.

Prayer for the Child of God

*F*ather, You sent Jesus to bind up _____'s heartaches and to heal his/her emotional and physical pain. The Bible says that You sent Your Word to heal him/her and to deliver _____ from all his/her destructions.

Lord, we believe; help our unbelief. We ask You to give _____ a spirit of wisdom and revelation [of insight into mysteries and secrets] in the [deep and intimate] knowledge of Jesus, the Messiah.

Father, as _____ grows in grace and the knowledge of the Lord Jesus Christ, help him/her to receive all the spiritual blessings given by You. Thank You for giving him/her peace that the world cannot take away.

Lord, Your Son, Jesus, gave His life for _____. He/she has received Him as his/her Lord and is born again, desiring to give the glory to You and to continue to fellowship with Your family. Jesus lives in his/her heart, and he/she loves You and loves others as he/she loves himself/herself. Thank You that _____ finds plenty of support from the Body of Christ so that he/she will find encouragement, edification and comfort.

Heavenly Father, in Your mercy strengthen _____ and help him/her with his/her physical problems. Let him/her be aware that he/she is not alone, for there is nothing that can separate him/her from the love of Christ—not pain or stress or persecution. He/she will come to the top of every circumstance or trial through Jesus' love.

Father, _____ is trusting in You and doing good; so shall he/she dwell in the land and feed surely on Your faithfulness, and truly he/she shall be fed. _____ delights himself/herself also in You, and You will give him/her the desires and secret petitions of his/her heart. We ask You to give _____ the grace to commit his/her way to You, trusting in You, and You will bring it to pass.

Help _____ to enter into Your rest, Lord, and to wait for You without fretting himself/herself. May he/she cease from unrighteous anger and wrath.

Father, You have not given _____ a spirit of fear, but of power and of love and of a sound mind. Neither shall he/she be confounded and depressed. You have given him/her beauty for ashes, the oil of joy for mourning and the garment of praise for the spirit of heaviness, that You might be glorified.

The chastisement [needful to obtain] _____'s peace and well-being was upon Jesus, and with the stripes [that wounded] Him, he/she was healed and made whole.

As Your child, Father, _____ has a joyful and confident hope of eternal salvation. This hope will never disappoint or delude him/her, for Your love has been poured out in his/her heart through the Holy Spirit, Who has been given to him/her.

In the name of Jesus, amen.

Scripture References

Luke 4:18 AMP	Romans 8:35-37
Psalm 107:20	2 Corinthians 2:14
Mark 9:24	Psalm 37:3-5,7,8 AMP
Ephesians 1:17 AMP	2 Timothy 1:7
2 Peter 3:18	Isaiah 54:4 AMP
Ephesians 1:3	Isaiah 61:3
John 14:27	Isaiah 53:5 AMP
John 3:3	Romans 5:4,5 AMP
John 13:34	

II.

Prayer for One Who Does Not Know Jesus As Lord

Thank You for calling us to be Your agents of intercession for _____. By the grace of God we will build up the wall and stand in the gap before You for _____, that he/she might be spared from eternal destruction.

Lord, we acknowledge Your Son, Jesus, as the Lamb of God, Who takes away _____'s sins. Thank You for sending the Holy Spirit, Who goes forth to convince and convict _____ of sin, righteousness and judgment. Your kindness leads him/her to repent (to change his/her mind and inner man to accept Your will). You are the One Who delivers _____ and draws him/her to Yourself out of the control and dominion of darkness and transfers him/her into the Kingdom of the Son of Your love.

Lord of the harvest, we ask You to thrust the perfect laborer into _____'s path, a laborer to share Your Gospel in a special way so that he/she will listen and understand it. We believe that he/she will come to his/her senses—come out of the snare of the devil who has held him/her captive—and make Jesus the Lord of his/her life.

Father, as _____ grows in grace and the knowledge of the Lord Jesus Christ, help him/her to receive all the spiritual blessings given by You. Thank You for giving him/her peace that the world cannot take away.

Heavenly Father, in Your mercy strengthen _____ and help him/her with his/her physical problems. Let him/her be aware that he/she is not alone, for there is nothing that can separate him/her from the love of Christ—not pain or stress or persecution. He/she will come to the top of every circumstance or trial through Jesus' love.

Help _____ to enter into Your rest and to wait for You without fretting himself/herself. May he/she cease from unrighteous anger and wrath.

Father, You sent Jesus to bind up _____'s heartaches and to heal his/her emotional and physical pain. The Bible says that You sent Your Word to heal him/her and to deliver _____ from all his/her destructions. We ask You to give him/her a spirit of wisdom and revelation [of insight into mysteries, and secrets] in the [deep and intimate] knowledge of Jesus, the Messiah.

The chastisement [needful to obtain] _____'s peace and well-being was upon Jesus, and with the stripes that wounded Him he/she was healed and made whole. As Your child, Father, _____ has a joyful and confident hope of eternal salvation. This hope will never disappoint or delude him/her, for Your love has been poured out in his/her heart through the Holy Spirit, Who has been given to him/her.

In the name of Jesus, amen.

Scripture References

Ezekiel 22:30 AMP

John 1:29

John 16:8-12 AMP

Romans 2:4 AMP

Colossians 1:13 AMP

Matthew 9:38 AMP

2 Timothy 2:26 NIV

2 Peter 3:18

Ephesians 1:3

John 14:27

Romans 8:35-37

2 Corinthians 2:14

Psalm 37:7,8 AMP

Luke 4:18 AMP

Psalm 107:20

Ephesians 1:17 AMP

Isaiah 53:5 AMP

Romans 5:5

58

Ministers to the Incarcerated

Introduction

*T*his prayer was written in response to a letter from an inmate. He had received Jesus, started a Bible study and wanted to know how to pray for God-called teachers and preachers to come and teach the inmates. He was praying for prisoners who did not know Jesus, believing that revival was coming to the correctional facility where he was housed.

Prayer

Father, You said that whoever calls upon the name of the Lord will be saved. How shall the inmates at this correctional facility/prison call on Him in Whom they have not believed? And how shall they believe in Him of Whom they have not heard? And how shall they hear without a preacher? And how shall they preach unless they are sent? We ask You, the Lord of the harvest, to send Your chosen laborers to preach deliverance to the captives of this prison.

Father, we thank You for Your ministers who are willing to go and preach deliverance to the incarcerated. May You grant to them out of the rich treasury of Your glory to be strengthened and reinforced with mighty power in the inner man by the [Holy] Spirit [Himself indwelling their innermost being and personality]. Anoint their lips to preach the good news of the Gospel.

Father, send Your Holy Spirit to go before the ministers, anoint the ears of the hearers and prepare their hearts to hear, receive, love and obey Your Word. Thank You that the light of the Gospel shines in their hearts so as to beam forth the light for the illumination of the knowledge of Your majesty and glory so that everyone who calls on Your name shall be saved.

Father, thank You for creating a desire within Your ministers to diligently study Your Word, that they might show themselves approved unto You, workmen who will not be put to shame, rightly dividing Your Word of truth. They are living witnesses to those who are not yet obedient to the Gospel.

Father, we thank You for an outpouring of Your Spirit upon the staff and inmates of this facility. We know that faith comes by hearing, and hearing by Your Word. We thank You for the salvation and deliverance of all those who call upon Your name.

In the name of Jesus, we thank You for sending the Holy Spirit, Who reveals truth to sinners, convicting and convincing them of sin, righteousness and judgment.

We release Your mercy, Your love and Your grace to those within these walls, that they might be saved through faith, and that not of themselves; it is Your gift.

Thank You, Lord, for hearing our prayer on behalf of the people at this correctional facility/prison.

In Jesus' name, amen.

Scripture References

Romans 10:13,14	*Romans 15:18*
Matthew 9:38	*Acts 2:18*
Ephesians 3:16 AMP	*Romans 10:17*
2 Corinthians 4:6 AMP	*John 16:8,13*
Romans 10:13	*Ephesians 2:8*
2 Timothy 2:15	

59

Prison Inmates

Introduction

*T*he following prayers were written in response to letters from prisoners requesting prayers to be used by them in special circumstances. They may be prayed in agreement with a prayer partner or intercessor.

I.

Prayer for an Inmate's Protection and Future

Father, I pray that I may become useful and helpful and kind to those around me, tenderhearted (compassionate, understanding, loving-hearted), forgiving others [readily and freely], as You, Father, in Christ forgave me my sins.

It is my desire to be an imitator of You, Lord. With the Holy Spirit as my Helper, I will [copy You and follow Your example], as a well-beloved child [imitates his/her father]. I purpose to walk in love, [esteeming and delighting in others] as Christ loves me. As I attend to Your Word, I depend on Your Holy Spirit to teach me to live a life of victory in Christ Jesus, my Lord.

In the name of Jesus, I am Your child. I am dwelling in the secret place of the Most High and abiding under the shadow of the Almighty. I say of You, Lord, that You are my Refuge and Fortress: my God; in You will I trust. You cover me with Your feathers, and under Your wings shall I trust: Your truth is my shield and buckler.

Because You are my Lord, my Refuge and Habitation, no evil shall befall me—no accident will overtake me—neither shall any plague or calamity come near me. You give Your angels [especial] charge over me, to keep me in all of my ways [of obedience and service].

Thank You for hearing my prayer. You are with me in trouble; You deliver me and satisfy me with long life and show me Your salvation.

In Jesus' name, amen.

Scripture References

Ephesians 4:32 AMP   *Psalm 91:9-11* AMP

Ephesians 5:1,2 AMP   *Psalm 91:15,16*

Psalm 91:1,2,4

II.

Prayer for an Incarcerated Parent and His/Her Children

Listen, God, I'm calling at the top of my lungs: "Be good to me! Answer me!"

When my heart whispered, "Seek God," my whole being replied, "I'm seeking Him!" Don't hide from me now.

I didn't know it before, but I know now that You've always been right here for me; don't turn Your back on me now. Don't throw me out; don't abandon me; You've always kept the door open.

Thank You for sending ministers to tell me about You and Your love for me.

My children say they hate me; they feel abandoned and alone. Even though their father/mother walked away from them, I ask You, Father, to take them in.

Lord of the harvest, I ask You to send laborers of the harvest and wise counselors to my children, who have been hurt by my actions.

Father, I have sinned against You, against my children and against myself. I repent of the sins that have so easily beset me and ask You to forgive me.

Father, Your Word assures me that You forgive me and cleanse me from all unrighteousness. Thank You for forgiving me. I pray that my children will be willing to forgive me so that we may be a family again.

In the name of Jesus, I cast the care of my children on You and rest in the assurance that You will perfect that which concerns me. I put on the garment of praise and delight myself in You. Teach me Your ways, O Lord, that I may walk and live in Your truth.

In Jesus' name, amen.

Scripture References

Psalm 27:7-10 MESSAGE	Psalm 138:8
Matthew 9:38	Isaiah 61:3
1 John 1:9	Psalm 37:4
1 Peter 5:7	Psalm 86:11 AMP

III.

Prayer for an Inmate To Pray for His/Her Family and Caregiver

Father, I have sinned against You, against my children and against myself. I repent of the sins that have so easily beset me, asking Your forgiveness.

Father, Your Word assures me that You forgive me and cleanse me from all unrighteousness. Thank You for forgiving me. I pray that my children will be willing to forgive me so that we may be a family again.

Thank You for the one who has assumed responsibility for my children while I am away. I pray that You will strengthen him/her and fill him/her with Your Spirit, Who gives him/her great wisdom, ability and skill in rearing the children You gave to me. I repent for failing to assume my responsibility to my children, and ask You to reward the one who is taking care of them.

His/her mouth shall speak of wisdom; and the meditation of his/her heart shall be understanding. I thank You that he/she is in Christ Jesus, Who has been made unto him/her wisdom from You—his/her righteousness, holiness and redemption. He/she is filled with the knowledge of Your will in all spiritual wisdom and understanding so that he/she may live a life worthy of You and may please You in every way, bearing fruit in every good work.

Father, I am responsible for my own actions, and I recognize that what I have done has hurt my entire family. Forgive me for dishonoring You, my family, my friends and my children. Give me the grace to pay my debt and do my assigned work as unto You. Help me to develop diligence and patience, giving myself to prayer, study and meditation in Your Word.

Lord, there is violence within these walls, but I look to You. Hide me in the secret place of Your presence from the plots of others. Keep me secretly in Your pavilion from the strife of tongues.

In the name of Jesus, I pray. Amen.

Scripture References

1 John 1:9	Colossians 1:9,10 AMP
Psalm 49:3	Colossians 3:23,24
1 Corinthians 1:30	Psalm 31:20

The Prayers of Jesus

The Prayers of Jesus

Matthew 6:9-13 AMP

Pray, therefore, like this: Our Father Who is in heaven, hallowed (kept holy) be Your name.

Your kingdom come, Your will be done on earth as it is in heaven.

Give us this day our daily bread.

And forgive us our debts, as we also have forgiven (left, remitted, and let go of the debts, and have given up resentment against) our debtors.

And lead (bring) us not into temptation, but deliver us from the evil one. *For Yours is the kingdom and the power and the glory forever. Amen.*

John 17:1-26 AMP

When Jesus had spoken these things, He lifted up His eyes to heaven and said, Father, the hour has come. Glorify and exalt and honor and magnify Your Son, so that Your Son may glorify and extol and honor and magnify You.

[Just as] You have granted Him power and authority over all flesh (all humankind), [now glorify Him] so that He may give eternal life to all whom You have given Him.

And this is eternal life: [it means] to know (to perceive, recognize, become acquainted with, and understand) You, the only true and real God, and [likewise] to know Him, Jesus [as the] Christ (the Anointed One, the Messiah), Whom You have sent.

I have glorified You down here on the earth by completing the work that You gave Me to do.

And now, Father, glorify Me along with Yourself and restore Me to such majesty and honor in Your presence as I had with You before the world existed.

I have manifested Your Name [I have revealed Your very Self, Your real Self] to the people whom You have given Me out of the world. They were Yours, and You gave them to Me, and they have obeyed and kept Your word.

Now [at last] they know and understand that all You have given Me belongs to You [is really and truly Yours].

For the [uttered words that You gave Me I have given them; and they have received and accepted [them] and have come to know positively and in reality [to believe with absolute assurance] that I came forth from Your presence, and they have believed and are convinced that You did send Me.

I am praying for them. I am not praying (requesting) for the world, but for those You have given Me, for they belong to You.

All [things that are] Mine are Yours, and all [things that are] Yours belong to Me; and I am glorified in (through) them. [They have done Me honor; in them My glory is achieved.]

And [now] I am no more in the world, but these are [still] in the world, and I am coming to You. Holy Father, keep in Your Name [in the knowledge of Yourself] those whom You have given Me, that they may be one as We [are one].

While I was with them, I kept and preserved them in Your Name [in the knowledge and worship of You]. Those You have given Me I guarded and protected, and not one of them has perished or is lost except the son of perdition [Judas Iscariot—the one who is now doomed to destruction, destined to be lost], that the Scripture might be fulfilled. [Ps. 41:9; John 6:70.]

And now I am coming to You; I say these things while I am still in the world, so that My joy may be made full and complete and perfect in them [that they may experience My delight fulfilled in them, that My enjoyment may be perfected in their own souls, that they may have My gladness within them, filling their hearts].

I have given and delivered to them Your word (message) and the world has hated them, because they are not of the world [do not belong to the world], just as I am not of the world.

I do not ask that You will take them out of the world, but that You will keep and protect them from the evil one.

They are not of the world (worldly, belonging to the world), [just] as I am not of the world.

Sanctify them [purify, consecrate, separate them for Yourself, make them holy] by Truth; Your Word is Truth.

Just as You sent Me into the world, I also have sent them into the world.

And so for their sake and on their behalf I sanctify (dedicate, consecrate) Myself, that they also may be sanctified (dedicated, consecrated, made holy) in the Truth.

Neither for these alone do I pray [it is not for their sake only that I make this request], but also for all those who will ever come to believe in (trust in, cling to, rely on) Me through their word and teaching,

That they all may be one, [just] as You, Father, are in Me and I in You, that they also may be one in Us, so that the world may believe and be convinced that You have sent Me.

I have given to them the glory and honor which You have given Me, that they may be one [even] as We are one:

I in them and You in Me, in order that they may become one and perfectly united, that the world may know and [definitely] recognize that You sent Me and that You have loved them [even] as You haved loved Me.

Father, I desire that they also whom You have entrusted to Me [as Your gift to Me] may be with Me where I am, so that they may see My glory, which You have given Me [Your love gift to Me]; for You loved Me before the foundation of the world.

O just and righteous Father, although the world has not known You and has failed to recognize You and has never acknowledged You, I have known you [continually]; and these men understand and know that You have sent Me.

I have made Your Name known to them and revealed Your character and Your very Self, and I will continue to make [You] known, that the love which You have bestowed upon Me may be in them [felt in their hearts] and that I [Myself] may be in them.

The Prayers of Paul

The Prayers of Paul

Ephesians 1:17-23 AMP

[For I always pray to] the God of our Lord Jesus Christ, the Father of glory, that He may grant you a spirit of wisdom and revelation [of insight into mysteries and secrets] in the [deep and intimate] knowledge of Him,

By having the eyes of your heart flooded with light, so that you can know and understand the hope to which He has called you, and how rich is His glorious inheritance in the saints (His set-apart ones),

And [so that you can know and understand] what is the immeasurable and unlimited and surpassing greatness of His power in and for us who believe, as demonstrated in the working of His mighty strength,

Which He exerted in Christ when He raised Him from the dead and seated Him at His [own] right hand in the heavenly [places],

Far above all rule and authority and power and dominion and every name that is named [above every title that can be conferred], not only in this age and in this world, but also in the age and the world which are to come.

And He has put all things under His feet and has appointed Him the universal and supreme Head of the church [a headship exercised throughout the church], [Ps. 8:6.]

Which is His body, the fullness of Him Who fills all in all [for in that body lives the full measure of Him Who makes everything complete, and Who fills everything everywhere with Himself].

Ephesians 3:14-21 AMP

For this reason [seeing the greatness of this plan by which you are built together in Christ], I bow my knees before the Father of our Lord Jesus Christ,

For Whom every family in heaven and on earth is named [that Father from Whom all fatherhood takes its title and derives its name].

May He grant you out of the rich treasury of His glory to be strengthened and reinforced with mighty power in the inner man by the [Holy] Spirit [Himself indwelling your innermost being and personality].

May Christ through your faith [actually] dwell (settle down, abide, make His permanent home) in your hearts! May you be rooted deep in love and founded securely on love,

That you may have the power and be strong to apprehend and grasp with all the saints [God's devoted people, the experience of that love] what is the breadth and length and height and depth [of it];

[That you may really come] to know [practically, through experience for yourselves] the love of Christ, which far surpasses mere knowledge [without experience]; that you may be filled [through all your being] unto all the fullness of God [may have the richest measure of the divine Presence, and become a body wholly filled and flooded with God Himself]!

Now to Him Who, by (in consequence of) the [action of His] power that is at work within us, is able to [carry out His purpose and] do superabundantly, far over and above all that we [dare] ask or think [infinitely beyond our highest prayers, desires, thoughts, hopes, or dreams]—

To Him be glory in the church and in Christ Jesus throughout all generations forever and ever. Amen (so be it).

Philippians 1:9-11 AMP

And this I pray: that your love may abound yet more and more and extend to its fullest development in knowledge and all keen insight [that your love may display itself in greater depth of acquaintance and more comprehensive discernment],

So that you may surely learn to sense what is vital, and approve and prize what is excellent and of real value [recognizing the highest and the best, and distinguishing the moral differences], and that you may be untainted and pure and unerring and blameless [so that with hearts sincere and certain and unsullied, you may approach] the day of Christ [not stumbling nor causing others to stumble].

May you abound in and be filled with the fruits of righteousness (of right standing with God and right doing) which come through Jesus Christ (the Anointed One), to the honor and praise of God [that His glory may be both manifested and recognized].

Colossians 1:9-12 AMP

For this reason we also, from the day we heard of it, have not ceased to pray and make [special] request for you, [asking] that you may be filled with the full (deep and clear) knowledge of His will in all spiritual wisdom [in comprehensive insight into the ways and purposes of God] and in understanding and discernment of spiritual things —

That you may walk (live and conduct yourselves) in a manner worthy of the Lord, fully pleasing to Him and desiring to please Him in all things, bearing fruit in every good work and steadily growing and increasing in and by the knowledge of God [with fuller, deeper, and clearer insight, acquaintance, and recognition].

[We pray] that you may be invigorated and strengthened with all power according to the might of His glory, [to exercise] every kind of endurance and patience (perseverance and forbearance) with joy,

Giving thanks to the Father, Who has qualified and made us fit to share the portion which is the inheritance of the saints (God's holy people) in the Light.

2 Thessalonians 1:11,12 AMP

With this in view we constantly pray for you, that our God may deem and count you worthy of [your] calling and [His] every gracious purpose of goodness, and with power may complete in [your] every particular work of faith (faith which is that leaning of the whole human personality on God in absolute trust and confidence in His power, wisdom, and goodness).

Thus may the name of our Lord Jesus Christ be glorified and become more glorious through and in you, and may you [also be glorified] in Him according to the grace (favor and blessing) of our God and the Lord Jesus Christ (the Messiah, the Anointed One).

MISSION STATEMENT

Word Ministries, Inc.

To motivate individuals to spiritual growth

and emotional wholeness,

encouraging them to become more deeply

and intimately acquainted

with the Father God

as they pray prayers that avail much.

About the Author

Germaine Griffin Copeland, founder and president of Word Ministries, Inc., is the author of the *Prayers That Avail Much* family of books. Her writings provide scriptural prayer instruction to help you pray effectively for those things that concern you and your family and for other prayer assignments. Her teachings on prayer, the personal growth of the intercessor, emotional healing and related subjects have brought understanding, hope, healing and liberty to the discouraged and emotionally wounded. She is a woman of prayer and praise whose highest form of worship is the study of God's Word. Her greatest desire is to know God.

Word Ministries, Inc. is a prayer and teaching ministry. Germaine believes that God has called her to teach the practical application of the Word of Truth for successful, victorious living. After years of searching diligently for truth and trying again and again to come out of depression, she decided that she was a mistake. Out of the depths of despair she called upon the name of the Lord, and the light of God's presence invaded the room where she was sitting.

It was in that moment that she experienced the warmth of God's love; old things passed away and she felt brand new. She discovered a motivation for living—life had purpose. Living in the presence of God she has found unconditional love and acceptance, healing for crippled emotions, contentment that overcomes depression, peace in the midst of adverse circumstances and grace for developing healthy relationships. The ongoing process of transformation evolved into praying for others, and the prayer of intercession became her prayer focus.

Germaine is the daughter of Reverend A. H. "Buck" Griffin and the late Donnis Brock Griffin. She and her husband, Everette, have four children, five grandchildren and two great-grandchildren. Germaine and Everette reside in Sandy Springs, a suburb of Atlanta, Georgia.

Word Ministries' offices are located in Historic Roswell, 38 Sloan Street, Roswell, Georgia 30075. Telephone: 770-518-1065.

You may contact
Word Ministries
by writing:

Word Ministries, Inc.
38 Sloan Street
Roswell, Georgia 30075
or calling 770-518-1065
www.prayers.org

Please include
your prayer requests
and comments when you write.

Other Books by Germaine Copeland

Prayers That Avail Much Journal

Prayers That Avail Much
WWJD Edition

Prayers That Avail Much Commemorative
Leather Edition

Prayers That Avail Much—Volume 1

Prayers That Avail Much—Volume 2

Oraciones Con Poder
Prayers That Avail Much
Spanish edition

Prayers That Avail Much Special Business Edition

Prayers That Avail Much—Special Edition
leather

Prayers That Avail Much for Mothers
pocket size

Prayers That Avail Much for Mothers
clothbound

Prayers That Avail Much Commemorative Gift Edition

Prayers That Avail Much for Men

Prayers That Avail Much for Women

Prayers That Avail Much for Teens
revised pocket edition

Prayers That Avail Much for Kids

Available from your local bookstore.

Harrison House
Tulsa, OK 74153

The Harrison House Vision

Proclaiming the truth and the power
Of the Gospel of Jesus Christ
With excellence;

Challenging Christians to
Live victoriously,
Grow spiritually,
Know God intimately.